1866 - 1991

125th

ANNIVERSARY

Your Barn House

Your Barn House

Hubbard and Betsy Cobb

Illustrations by Mary Lohmann
Photographs by Tom Hopkins unless otherwise noted

Henry Holt and Company New York

Published by Henry Holt and Company, Inc.,
115 West 18th Street, New York, New York 10011.
Published in Canada by Fitzhenry & Whiteside Limited,
195 Allstate Parkway, Markham, Ontario L3R 4T8.

Library of Congress Cataloging-in-Publication Data
Cobb, Hubbard H.
    Your barn house / Hubbard and Betsy Cobb.—1st ed.
        p.   cm.
    Includes bibliographical references and index.
    ISBN 0-8050-1151-X
    1. Dwellings.   2. Barns—Remodeling for other use.   I. Cobb,
Betsy.   II. Title.
TH4812.C6   1991
690′.837—dc20   90-20293
                                                 CIP

Henry Holt books are available at special discounts
for bulk purchases for sales promotions, premiums,
fund-raising, or educational use. Special editions
or book excerpts can also be created to specification.
For details contact:
Special Sales Director, Henry Holt and Company, Inc.
115 West 18th Street, New York, New York 10011
First Edition

BOOK DESIGN BY CLAIRE NAYLON VACCARO

Printed in the United States of America
Recognizing the importance of preserving
the written word, Henry Holt and Company, Inc.,
by policy, prints all of its first editions
on acid-free paper. ∞
10 9 8 7 6 5 4 3 2 1

Disclaimer

The contents of this book are presented in good faith and with many cautionary suggestions as to safety for those attempting any of the procedures described herein. Since much of the material recounts the experience of others as told to us, the authors cannot assume responsibility for any direct or indirect loss or injury from actions taken as a result of reading this book. Listing of timber framers, manufacturers of kits, or any products mentioned are not to be taken as recommendations by the authors, but rather are presented as information only, to be followed up and acted upon at the discretion of the reader. Variations in skills and physical condition and regional differences in climate and price must also be taken into consideration.

Contents

Acknowledgments

Before we begin our separate thank-yous to the many individuals who have given so generously of their expertise, knowledge, and experience during the researching and compiling of this book, we'd like to mention a discovery we made along the way—that those who are deeply involved with barns, whether in the business of giving old barns new lives, building new barns into houses, or presently living in their own barn houses, are exceptionally nice people, and we feel fortunate to have had the opportunity to meet and work with them. Sometimes these meetings have been accomplished through long and productive telephone conversations, more often in person. In each instance, they did their best to answer our numerous questions and fulfill our many requests for information, floor plans, old photographs, and the hundreds of other details that went into the making of this book. We salute them all and deeply appreciate their cooperation.

To these timber framers and post-and-beam builders, we owe our special thanks—we learned so much from you.

Ken Epworth, Susan Fuller, David Hill; The Barn People
Alex Greenwood; New Jersey Barn Company

Patsy and Pat Hennin; The Shelter Institute
Judith Landau; Timbercraft
John Libby; Barn Masters
Fred Miller; New Hampshire
Anita Haines Roberts; Peg and Beam
Craig Rowley; Restorations Ltd.
Terry Turney; Pacific Post and Beam
Wil Wilkins; Timberhouse

To the following building professionals, architects, and others who were especially helpful to us—thank you very much.

John Bogaert; Bogaert Construction Company, Inc.
Philip Casker; Casker Design and Construction Company
Chad Floyd, Nancy King; Centerbrook Architects
John Lyon; Atlas Industries
Jim Maynard; Essex Plumbing Company, Inc.
Janet Null; Argus Architecture and Preservation
Kathy Short; *Successful Farming* magazine
James P. Warfield; School of Architecture, University of Illinois at
    Urbana-Champaign

To each of those who allowed us to tell the story of how their barn house came to be—our deep appreciation and thanks for your generosity in sharing your experience with us and our readers.

To our agent, Elizabeth Knappman, who sparked to the idea of *Your Barn House* when we first suggested it, found the right publisher, and cheered and encouraged us when we thought, because of momentum lost after an automobile accident, we'd never be able to finish the book, our gratitude and appreciation. To our good friend Joyce Winston, whose early explorations into the fine old barns of Pennsylvania contributed much to our concept of how the book should be developed, our admiration and deep appreciation. And to Tracy Bernstein, our editor, whose patience and understanding in extending our deadline more than twice, and for bearing with grace our stretched-out delivery of manuscript, illustrations, and photographs—our gratitude and sincere thanks.

Introduction

Americans love barns. We love to look at them as we drive along country roads. We love to look at pictures of barns, to photograph them, to paint them.

Barns are part of our heritage, probably the purest form of American architecture. They are honest, functional structures, originally built for the most basic of reasons—to provide safe, dry shelter for domestic animals and for crops. Early settlers in New England and pioneer families in the Midwest built their barns before their homes. They lived in crude cabins or sod houses nearby or sometimes shared their barns with their horses and cows until circumstances permitted the building of a house as fine and sturdy as their barn.

Today, many of us would choose the barn—whether an antique barn converted into a dwelling or a barn house newly built with the exposed frame, heavy timbers, and structural integrity that made the early barns so appealing. The possibilities offered by a barn's interior are infinite. Since the frame alone supports the entire structure, there is no need for load-bearing walls and, except for working around the *center posts* that are required in the interior of most barns, there is total freedom to allocate the space in any way you wish.

We will show you how twenty barn house owners have divided their spaces to make homes for themselves. Each of these barn houses is different. Some cost considerable money; others, though modest in cost, are lavish in talent, both professional and amateur. With a lot of intensive labor and dedication to the job, they have been made into cherished and totally unique homes. Throughout this book you will find many ideas and helpful suggestions, so that you may go about fulfilling your own barn house aspirations with confidence, and with enough foreknowledge of the possible perils and pitfalls that—with luck—you will avoid them all.

Your Barn House

New England barn. (Illustration by Mary Lohmann.)

CHAPTER ONE

Evolution of the American Barn

The barns built by colonists in the New World in the mid-1600s were made of logs, and could conceivably be called the first truly American barns. These log barns remained popular for many generations and can still be found in some parts of the country, especially in the Appalachians, parts of the Southeast, Indiana, and Texas.

When the early settlers got around to building more elaborate barns, the design and construction were much the same as those of farm buildings in the countries of their origin. In New England, for example, English settlers first built their barns of half-timbers with "cod," a mixture of clay and straw, set between the timbers. Roofs were of thatch, just as they were back home, and interiors were modeled after the three-bay barn common in sixteenth-century England. But the cod-and-thatch construction suitable for the milder English climate did not stand up to the harsh New England winters and was soon replaced by wood siding and shingle roofs. The three-bay interior design was practical, however, and became more or less standard. It was now popularly known as the English or Yankee barn.

Dutch farmers, settling in New York State along the Hudson River in the sixteenth and seventeenth centuries, modeled their handsome barns after traditional farm buildings in the Netherlands. These barns are large, soundly built, and efficient, and are regarded today as architectural gems. Their outstanding feature is the steeply pitched roof so well suited to the climate of the New World.

German farmers settling in Pennsylvania, and mistakenly called Pennsylvania Dutch (from "Deutsch"), built most of their barns with limestone, which was easy to work and could be found in abundant supply in the area. This, and the more common fieldstone, soon became the favorite material not only for barns but for houses, too. Roof rafters, floor joists, and beams, as in the all-wood English and Dutch barns, were built with large hand-hewn timbers connected by wood joinery.

Many of these barns had two floors and were set into a slope or an embankment, with an entrance on either side. Hay wagons and other farm vehicles had easy access to the wide barn doors built into the upper level; the lower or ground level opened on a large, airy barnyard and contained the stalls where the livestock were kept at night. These structures were called bank barns and are so practical that they are used not only in Pennsylvania but in many other parts of the country as well.

Wherever they built their barns, whether in Pennsylvania, New England, or elsewhere, early farmers were always aware of the importance of good orientation. They would carefully site their structures in accordance

New world Dutch barn. (Illustration by Mary Lohmann.)

Pennsylvania barn. (Illustration by Mary Lohmann.)

with the prevailing wind. This usually meant that the barnyard faced south for the protection of the animals and that the advice given in an old New England *Farmer's Almanac* to "slope your barn against the Northern blast" was heeded. Windows are few on most barns, especially on the north side, in order to conserve heat in cold weather.

In parts of northern New England, where winters are long, harsh, and bitter, farmers wisely took their own well-being—as well as the animals'—into consideration, and joined the barn and other farm buildings to the house, so that they could do chores in cold weather without having to face the elements. This arrangement is called a "continuous barn." Unfortunately, it was also a fire hazard, for a fire in one building could quickly spread and engulf an entire complex.

The attractive cupolas we see on many barns are not just for decorative purposes; they are there to provide ventilation and to release heat generated by livestock, stored hay, and other farm produce. Early silos were not the tall, cylindrical structures we see today, but instead holes dug into the ground and lined with stone. Covered, they were used to store corn and other feed grains. The towering silos we are familiar with came into use around the 1870s.

Bank barn. (Illustration by Mary Lohmann.)

Some barns, usually relatively small, were designed for a single purpose—to store hay, a wagon, or farm equipment; or to house cows or horses. But a large barn could handle all this and more under one roof and still have space left over for a few sheep and hogs. Before the development of the combine, for instance, a barn would often include a "threshing floor" where grain was flailed by hand to separate the wheat from the chaff. Bins to store grain and straw lined each side of the threshing floor.

All barns built in the eighteenth and early nineteenth centuries were constructed of solid timbers connected by mortise-and-tenon, dovetail, half-lap, and other joinery techniques. Timbers were held together and secured with wooden pegs driven in with a heavy mallet called a beetle. Colonial houses were built in the same way, but the structural timbers, exposed in the barn, were covered with plaster or paneling in a home so that the fine details of the wooden joinery were usually hidden from view.

Around 1830, waves of farmers started migrating to the fertile mid-

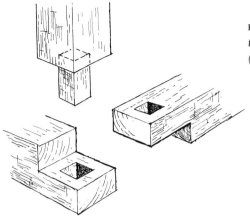

HALF-LAP: *Sills joined at corner with half-lap mortises so tenon at end of post secures half-lap and fixes post to sills. (Illustration by Mary Lohmann.)*

DOVETAIL: *Dovetail joint secures floor beams to sills. Dovetails can be found on much fine wood furniture. (Illustration by Mary Lohmann.)*

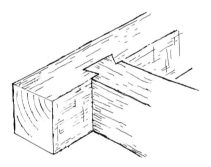

FLOOR FRAME: *Floor frame of old barn includes fieldstone foundations, main girder, floor beams, and floor planks. It was common practice not to nail floor planks in place until barn frame had been erected. (Illustration by Mary Lohmann.)*

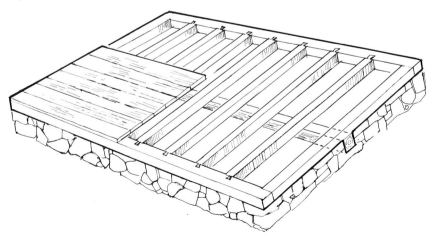

Prairie barn. (Illustration by Mary Lohmann.)

western lands. They were in need of houses and barns that could be erected quickly. At that time, two important innovations came about that were to affect building methods for the next 150 years. These were the vastly more efficient sawmills, which could slice a log into boards 1⅝ inch thick in jig time, and the mass production of factory-made wire nails that would join the boards together. Buildings could now be assembled not only quickly but with less skill and experienced labor. So as the old ways were being abandoned, "stud" or "stick-built" construction came into general use.

Utilizing these new methods, enormous barns were built to accommodate the huge crops being produced by farmers with constantly improving mechanical equipment. These "temples of abundance," as they have been called, attested not only to the fertility of the soil but to the tireless efforts of the farmer, his entire family, and his hired hands.

As the nineteenth century rolled along, new barn designs came into being. Prominent among them was the Shaker round barn, a beautiful, highly efficient building that filled many different functions. It was complicated to build, however, and began to be superceded by the octagonal barn, a modification that was somewhat easier to build, though still more difficult than a rectangular structure. Most of these later barns were mainly stud construction, but they, too, along with the prairie barn and the western barn, became American classics.

Gambrel roof barn. (Illustration by Mary Lohmann.)

By the close of the nineteenth century, only a few barns using the timber frame method were being built. So this ancient craft, used since the twelfth century in Europe and for millennia in the Far East, fell into disuse in this country and almost became extinct.

The many Colonial houses still gracing our landscape today are there because they were well maintained or have been lovingly restored. The same cannot be said of old barns. While there are old barns still standing—sturdy monuments to those early barn builders—far too many others have been allowed to disintegrate and collapse, or have simply been razed in the name of progress.

The twentieth century, especially the latter half, saw countless old barns torn down. Unable to compete with the large agricultural enterprises that had begun to feed the nation, small family farms began to disappear at an alarming rate; along with them went the traditional barns that were an integral part of the family farmstead. Urbanization raced along, farmland was sold off, and barns were demolished to make way for housing developments, shopping centers, and industrial parks.

Even on those family farms still operating, changes in agricultural practices seemingly made the old barn unnecessary—it was cheaper to house new farm machinery in quickly erected metal sheds than to spend the money to put a new roof on the old barn. Allowed to fall into disrepair, roofs caved in, moisture and rot took their toll, and the once-sturdy structures continued to collapse. In some communities, if the old wreck hadn't quite given way, local fire departments were invited by the owner to burn it down—thus getting rid of the barn and giving firemen experience at the same time. (Today, antipollution laws in many states bar this practice.)

From the mid-sixties on through the seventies, popular interest in the use of exposed timbers and vaulted or "cathedral" ceilings burgeoned. A few forward-looking manufacturers in the cabinetmaking and home-building fields, sensing the public's desire for more natural environments and more individualistic homes than the look-alike houses then available, began to market packaged houses—post-and-beam kits using new timbers. Interestingly, many of these packaged kits were designed as barn houses or barn-style houses. At least one of these manufacturers also offered weathered timbers and boards from actual old barns and other structures that had been dismantled. Since hand-crafted mortise-and-tenon joinery was so time-consuming, newer ways of connecting and supporting structural members were devised; these included lag screws, long nails, and metal hangers. Public response to the packaged houses was enthusiastic and the industry has thrived. Many more companies have entered the field, some of them now using sophisticated machinery to produce the mortise-and-tenon joinery traditionally hewn by hand.

The past decade or so has also seen an awakening of interest in the renovation of antique braced-frame timber structures—especially barns. A number of restorationists, craftspeople, and young builders interested in preserving historic buildings became concerned about the thousands of antique barns that were falling into ruin, or were slated for demolition. Some of these old barns could be had just for the carting away, others for a couple of hundred dollars or so. They began rescuing the old structures and rebuilding them elsewhere. Barns sound enough to be moved were carefully dismantled—the timbers numbered and coded in the exact order of disassembly—then trucked to the shop, where they would be cleaned, repaired if necessary, and restored; ready to be re-erected on new foundations into comfortable, and often luxurious, homes. (This practice has created considerable controversy among historians and others interested in preserving these symbols of the past in the pure form of their original use.)

During this dismantling and rebuilding, much was learned about the old techniques of wood joinery. Some artisan-craftspeople, eager to learn more about this ancient way of building so long ignored in this country, traveled to Europe and also to Japan, where master carpenters still practice traditional timber frame skills. They came home inspired and found kindred souls among their peers who were also eager to build enduring structures in which they could take lasting pride.

In 1985, a group of about two hundred of these timber framers formed the Timber Framers Guild of North America, dedicated to sustaining the highest standards of the craft. Through seminars, workshops, national and regional conferences, and the publication of a newspaper, the guild has spread the timber frame message and now, at the beginning of the 1990s, has over 750 members. Some bring their skills to building structures of all kinds—including commercial enterprises. Others specialize in the conversion of antique frames—especially barns—into houses. Still others, finding the old barns harder and harder to come by, and trying to keep costs down for prospective homeowners, are building barn house frames the old way, but with new timbers.

So, the more things change, the more they remain—almost—the same. The wheel has come full circle.

BARE BONES OF BARN CONSTRUCTION

Barns, whether old or new, are seldom framed in exactly the same fashion, but all will include most of these basic elements.

1. *Sills*: Timbers set horizontally on top of the foundation wall into which the vertical posts and floor beams are set. Today, sills are secured to the foundation with anchor bolts.

2. *Girder or Main Beam*: A heavy timber that provides support for the floor beams and intermediate posts. A girder (or girders) may run either the width or length of the structure.

3. *Floor Beams or Floor Joists*: Timbers that support the floor. The ends of these beams may rest on the sills or be set into the sills. They are given support by the girder, or girders.

4. *Posts*: Vertical timbers that are a principal element of the frame.

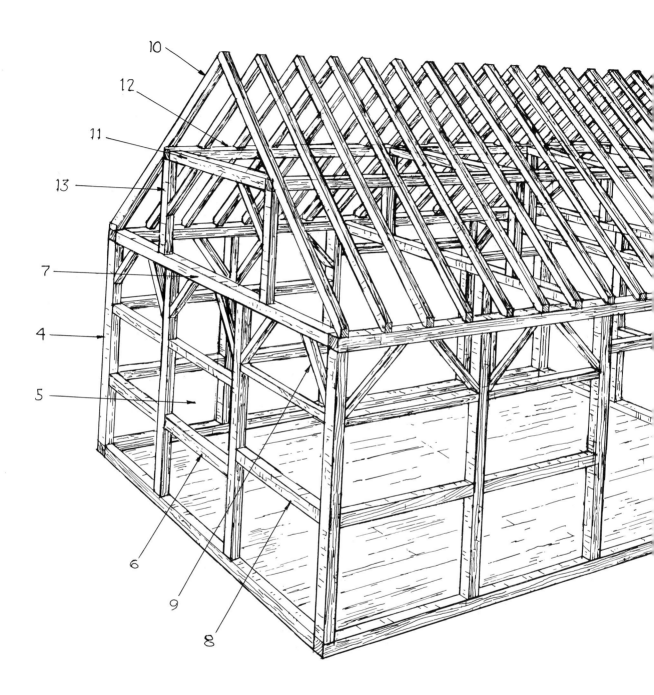

(Illustrations by Mary Lohmann [adapted from a drawing by The Barn People].)

5.   *Bent*: A structural assembly of timbers that makes up one cross-sectional element of the frame. There are numerous variations of the bent, depending on the size and complexity of the building. Sometimes roof rafters are incorporated into a bent. In its most simple form, a bent consists of two posts connected at the top by a horizontal timber. Bents are often assembled on the ground, fitted and pegged, then lifted into place either manually or by a crane. Bents are usually spaced no more than sixteen feet apart, and the space between the bents is called a bay.

6.   *Girts*: Horizontal timbers that connect the posts.

7.   *Bent Girt*: The girt that connects the posts in a single bent.

8.   *Connecting Girt*: A girt that connects posts of one bent to the posts of the other bents. There may be several connecting girts, depending on the height of the posts.

9.   *Knee Braces*: Short lengths of timber set diagonally to reinforce the joints between posts and girts.

10.   *Roof Rafters*: Timbers that frame the roof. The upper ends of rafters are sometimes joined with a "ridgepole"—a horizontal timber run-

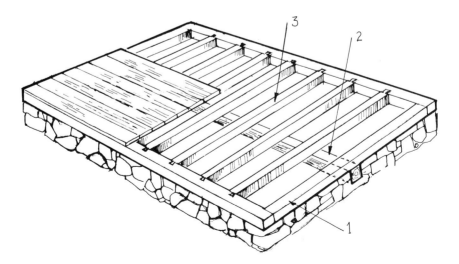

ning the length of the roof. The base, or "heel," of the rafters may rest on the connecting girts or on a horizontally set timber called a plate.

11. *Collar Tie*: A timber used to connect a pair of rafters. With very long rafters there may be two collar ties—a short one near the peak of the roof and another one lower down.

12. *Purlin*: A timber (commonly 4-by-4 inch to 6-by-6 inch) running longitudinally, perpendicular to, or across and "let in" to the rafters to serve as nailing and support for roof sheathing.

13. *Queen Posts*: A pair of posts set on top of a bent girt that provides support to collar ties, purlin, and rafters.

14. *Strut* (not shown): A short timber often set under the purlin to assist in transferring the load imposed on the purlin to other parts of the frame. If the roof is very broad and maximum strength is required to handle heavy snow, the strut may be incorporated with other timbers to form a "truss."

15. *Summer Beam* (not shown): A large timber that connects the bent girts usually at or near the midpoint of their span. Sometimes serves as a girder to support the beams that frame the second floor, but primarily supports or carries one end of the floor joists. On a very wide building, there may be two or more summer beams.

CHAPTER TWO

Seven Ways to Get a Barn House of Your Own

We talk a lot in this book about the disappearance of old barns, along with the disappearance of the small family farm. There are still old barns to be had but they are harder to find, and in some parts of the country they can be impossible to find. Yet, if your heart is set on a barn house, there are ways to get one. The key is to stay flexible—there are many roads to a barn house.

1. Buy a House with a Barn

This can make sense for many reasons. It is easier to find a house that has a barn on the property than to find just a barn. It's also easier to get financing for the purchase if there is a house involved. Mortgage lenders can be very skittish if asked to lend money on an empty barn that has yet to be made into a house. Today, especially after the S&L debacle, mortgage money is hard to find. The fact that a property you like includes a house is a definite plus.

With a house/barn combination you have several options.

You can sell or rent the house.

You can live in the house yourself while the barn is being renovated. The advantage here is that you're right on the spot when decisions have to be made.

You can provide your parents with a place of their own that would be close enough so you could keep an eye on them.

You can move the barn to a more desirable location on the property (assuming there are no objections from the local zoning board).

You could sell off some of the land, with or without the house, as Jill Butler did (see page 117). This could give you some cash reserve to help pay for the barn renovation.

You might decide to live in the house yourself and use the barn for other purposes—guest house, office, workshop, studio. A family in Pennsylvania created a roomy in-law apartment on the second (loft) level of their barn, adding an outside staircase in the rear. The barn was so large that they could, at the same time, stable two horses in the remaining space with plenty of room for hay. (This practice—humans and animals under the same roof—is not legal in all states; California, for one.)

2. Buy Just the Barn

This is the dream of many, but it can also be the most difficult. First, you have to find a suitable barn and it must be in good condition. Then the owner must be persuaded that selling is a good idea. If you're lucky, the owner has no practical use for the barn and would be willing to sell it, along with a parcel of land. Chances are, though, that the barn is

14

too close to the owner's house. The local zoning board may object to this, and so, too, may you, from the standpoint of privacy. If the barn has to be moved for whatever reason, you are in for a sizable expense (see chapter 7).

Buying just the barn can be tricky to finance, as we said earlier. You might, however, be able to work out some form of so-called creative financing with the seller, where he or she takes back a mortgage until you feel you are far enough along with the project to have a solid case to present to a bank for a construction loan. Otherwise, you'll have to come up with the cash. Nonetheless, if the barn is just what you want and can be had for a reasonable price, it can be well worth the time, effort, and money to go ahead and buy it.

3. Buy a Barn and Move It to Your Site

Occasionally you might run into a situation where an owner is willing to sell or even give away a barn, provided it is removed from the property and all debris is removed along with it. This might be because the area is being cleared, perhaps for development or for a road. It's the sort of thing that happened much more often in the past, but now there are fewer barns and more people aware of their possible historic or monetary value.

If you happen to be in the right place at the right time, you might hear of something like that—but you'd have to act fast. This means you should have a qualified person in mind who could take charge of such a project. Who you have depends on the type of barn—post-and-beam timber frame, or stud-built. If the former, we suggest a timber framer or restorationist—if the latter, a master carpenter or a house mover experienced with barns. John Libby of Barn Masters, Inc. of Freeport, Maine, was recently faced with just such a situation.

An antique 40-by-50-foot barn was scheduled to be demolished by a building crew and bulldozer. A "neighbor to the barn" who was also a good friend of Libby's told him the barn was being taken down. John contacted the person demolishing the barn and found that there was a deadline of four weeks, at which time the barn was to be gone from the site and all debris removed. He then contacted two prospective clients, one of whom said he would take the barn.

John and his timber frame crew dismantled the barn in two weeks. "Labeling each timber, knee brace, etc., we transported it forty miles to another town and had a wonderful barn raising. It took four days to assemble the bents, and two days to raise the frame. The barn is now used to house livestock, equipment, vehicles, and to eventually complement a house that has yet to be designed."

This barn was moved, of course, under pressure of time. It pays to get the names of people who are experienced in moving and/or dismantling barns, and, if possible, check them out and meet them, at the same time you're looking for the actual barn. Aside from being prepared to move quickly, you will also now have another avenue opened to you. Professionals who are involved with old barns or other historic structures keep up with the barn grapevine and know, or are apt to hear, as John Libby did, about available barns. Also, timber framers may very well have in their inventory just the barn you are searching for. Which leads us into the next way we suggest you get your own barn.

4. Buy an Antique Barn Frame

If what you want is a barn with a history—an eighteenth- or early-nineteenth-century post-and-beam structure—and you don't have the time to spend searching for one, look for a timber framer or restorationist who buys and sells old barns. A big advantage to working with experienced people like these is that if you buy a dismantled frame from them you will have the assurance that the timbers are sound—and that they have been cleaned, repaired, and properly marked so that they can be readily reassembled and re-erected. Also, they will re-erect the frame on your site.

A timber frame firm often has an inventory of old barns—some of them already dismantled and with parts repaired, ready to reassemble for a client. Occasionally they will be able to show you barns still standing, ready to be dismantled. In this case, they will have made some kind of agreement with the owner to take the barn down. Such barns, if they are really old—or if they are historic gems—won't be available for long. If the former, they will continue to deteriorate, unless repaired, an expense the owner probably would not undertake. If they are true gems, they'll likely be spotted and snapped up by a historic barn lover.

Fred Miller, a timber framer and barn expert from Colebrook, New Hampshire, showed us pictures of several barns in his inventory—a couple of them still standing, others in the process of being disassembled. Fred is a real barn buff (as are most timber framers) and really goes into the history of each barn he deems worthy. One of particular historic interest had been used in pre–Civil War days as part of an underground stopover for slaves escaping to Canada and freedom. His part of northern New Hampshire is very close to the Canadian border, as were the barns he described to us.

Fred provides the buyer of one of his barns with a history of the barn and detailed drawings of the frame. He will also build a scale model of the frame, so the buyer can better plan how to allocate space in the barn-house-to-be. (Several other timber framers also do this. Just ask.) The scale model really helps and is also nice to have around once your barn house is finished.

Another timber framer who handles only antique barn frames is Alex Greenwood of the New Jersey Barn Company in Princeton, New Jersey. His inventory is limited (as most such inventories are—there are just not that many available). Most of the barns he handles are in the English or New World Dutch framing traditions and are massively framed structures made of oak (see sources).

In the East and Northeast, the price of an antique barn frame runs around $40 a square foot, including erection of the frame. Usually the charge will also cover delivery of the frame within a radius of a hundred miles or less. Shipping charges beyond a stated distance are extra, but they are not so terribly high that it wouldn't be worth your while to ship much farther. Some firms handling both antique and new frames ship loaded flatbed trucks from the East Coast to California and all points in between.

Pennsylvania is another eastern state where timber framers are active in restoring old barns and dismantling, moving, and re-erecting them. Several also build new timber frames. Brian Murphy Barn Restorations of Ottsville, Pennsylvania, specializes in Pennsylvania bank barns. He deals with antique barns only, mostly in the Bucks County area. The Timber Framers Guild of North America Directory (see sources) lists these companies and many in other states.

Most dealers in old frames will see the project through to delivery and erection of the frame only. A few will offer additional assistance in planning or working with your contractor or architect toward completion of the barn house. The cost of completing your barn house can run from $50 to $150 or more a square foot, depending on how luxurious a place you want, how much finish work you do yourself, and which section of the country you are in. You also have to figure in architect's or designer's fees. These costs, of course, are in addition to the initial cost of the frame.

5. Buy a New Barn Frame

This is a fine approach if you don't insist on an antique barn. In fact, because of the scarcity of old barns, many timber framers who began with the renovation or dismantling of antique barns now offer the same expertise in the building of new frames. Craig Rowley Restorations of Amston, Connecticut, is one of these (see page 117). In addition to his restoration work, Rowley offers a 26-by-36-foot precrafted timber frame of oak, with mortise-and-tenon joints and wood pegs, shipped and erected on your foundation. His starting rate is $25 a square foot. With this type of firm you can still have handcrafted joinery, large timbers, and your frame put together and raised in the traditional way.

Some of the larger companies that offer new frames will work with you and/or your contractor or architect to adapt their stock plans to fit your requirements. Others will work from your plans or your architect's. They will help you make decisions and choices; orient your structure for the best possible natural light, energy conservation, and solar heat gain; and so on. Their design and architectural staffs will do blueprints and construction drawings for you and they will do their best to stay within your budget requirements, promising no large cost overruns.

They will build you a barn house frame, large or small. One company in the far West, Timberhouse Post & Beam in Victor, Montana, is presently building a fishing and hunting lodge in Jackson Hole, Wyoming, under the architectural direction of world-renowned architect Cesar Pelli, that will run well over 10,000 square feet. Another project will exceed 55,000. This does not mean, however, that a small structure is of no interest to them. Wil Wilkins, the president of the company, emphasizes the firm's dedication to quality and the fact that each house is as unique, and important to them, as it is to the client. They will be happy to work with you in constructing your barn house frame of only 1,000 square feet, if that is what you want, and what your budget limitations are. Depending on the size of the timbers used, and the "embellishments," as timber framers call chamfered edges, curved braces, and other special touches added to the timbers, prices for a frame wrapped in stress-skin panels start at $27 to $30 a square foot.

Some timber framers just do frames. Others, like Timberhouse Post & Beam, will make the frame weathertight, usually with stress-skin panels. And many will complete the house. Timbercraft Homes in Port Townsend, Washington, handled Nancy Franken's entire project—from helping her develop the plans to erecting the frame and completing the house down to the last detail (see page 93). This custom home-building service is offered to residents of the Puget Sound area only, but the company's design, engineering, and consulting services are available to clients in any area.

6. Buy a Precut-Package Manufactured Barn House

This can be a quick and efficient way to get your own post-and-beam barn house. And you can have just about any size, style, and layout that you want. The larger manufacturers have design staffs that will work with you to adapt any of their basic standard plans to suit your needs. If, for instance, you want to add a downstairs bedroom and bath to a standard living room/dining room/kitchen plan, as Paula Landesmann did when she decided to order a Yankee Barn Homes package, you can have the manufacturer's plan easily customized by the design staff using sophisticated electronic equipment (called CAD—for "computer-assisted design"). This equipment saves countless hours in creating new designs and in making adjustments and changes. (Yankee Barn Homes, by the way, is one of the oldest manufacturers in the business, and from their Grantham, New Hampshire, headquarters can offer clients either new timbers for their barn houses or resawn antique timbers stockpiled from old mills, factories, and other early buildings.)

Other manufactured, precut barn house packages, in addition to offering their own standard plans, will work with your plans or those of your architect or designer to give you an entirely custom-made package. All timbers will be cut to your specifications and joinery will be precision engineered to assure exact fit when assembled. Some companies offer hand-finished joinery with mortises and tenons and wood pegs, and some use half-lap joints or metal fasteners to assemble the posts and beams.

Lary Bloom and Elizabeth Gwillim had their own architect design the exact barn house they wanted (see page 81). The package was then produced for them by Habitat/American Barn working closely with their architect. It was delivered to their site complete with windows and doors, roofing, siding, decking, flooring, and all materials needed for an insulated, weathertight shell. The owners were responsible only for appliances, cabinetry, and finish work—along with, of course, engaging a contractor to put the shell together.

Most manufacturers of precut package houses—whether barn houses or others—do not erect the frame. But they will sometimes send a company representative to supervise the erection of the frame, as did Timberpeg, the New Hampshire company that precut the very specialized barn house designed by architect Janet Null for Jenifer and Fuller Cowles in Minnesota (see page 159). This most unusual plan called for a timber frame 72 foot long by 34 foot wide. Included in this vast space is a two-story 34-by-36-foot studio, where the oversized sculptures of Fuller Cowles are created. In this instance, Timberpeg supplied only the frame and the expertise to engineer it. The company, however, usually offers a complete package to the client, as do most other manufacturers of precut packages.

Many packagers include everything required for a weathertight shell—frame, sheathing, insulation, siding, roofing, windows, exterior doors, and subflooring. Others, in addition, provide materials for much of the finish work—trim, flooring, stairs, balconies, railings, and so on. The catalog and literature from each manufacturer will list exactly what is included in their particular package.

One of the several advantages to buying a packaged barn house is that you will know what the total cost will be. There are seldom cost overruns, unless something entirely unexpected occurs—usually on your building site—such as problems with septic system installation or with your contractor or a subcontractor. (Some precut barn house manufacturers are listed in the sources section. You will also find books on factory-made and manufactured houses listed in the bibliography.)

7. Build It Yourself from a Kit

This is the way to go if your taste level is higher than your bank account—and if you have the time, energy, and dedication to undertake what can only be described as a *big* job.

Your best bet here is to buy a post-and-beam kit—preferably from an outfit that will erect the frame on your site. This will still leave you with plenty of work to do. Nancy and Gary Miers bought their frame components in a kit made up by The Shelter Institute, which erected the frame for them on their foundation (see page 97).

Tom Hopkins, on the other hand, bought his frame kit from a company that delivered the timbers to the site and had nothing to do with helping erect it. Tom was fortunate in that his crew of three included an experienced carpenter/brother, but even so, they had to hire a crane to lift the roof rafters into place.

Shelter-Kit, Inc. of Tilton, New Hampshire, has been building kits for various types of houses for more than twenty years. These kits are expressly designed for assembly by people who have never had construction experience. According to reports about the company, Shelter-Kit's directions are written clearly and explicitly and no owner has ever been unable to complete a house. Encouraging news.

The company now produces a Barn-House Kit that contains all the lumber, hardware, roofing, and instructions needed to build a weathertight shell. All lumber for this kit is precut, except for the upper siding. Construction of the kit is part post and beam and part stud, which is used for exterior walls. It is a factory modification of the firm's regular Barn Kit, which is entirely post and beam. Andy Prokosch, the company's president, believes that stud wall construction is simpler for the first-time builder to insulate, since sheathing is installed on the exterior walls with insulation applied between studs in the conventional manner. A Barn-House Kit for a 24-by-24-foot structure with windows, doors, and stairs included can be had for $14,885 (see sources).

Using an Architect or Designer

Whether you are renovating a barn or building your barn house from a frame, either old or new, we suggest having an architect or architectural designer draw up your plans. Even though using such a professional is an additional expense, in the long run you'll save time and money and end up with a better result.

If you are building from a new or antique frame, your architect will, no doubt, want to consult with, and work with, the timberwright(s) who will be erecting the frame. If you are working with a precut package manufacturer, again, your architect will want to consult with the company's design and engineering staffs.

Several people we write about in this book have converted their barn houses themselves, without benefit of architectural advice and guidance and with admirable results. Nevertheless, if you can swing it, we say use an architect or architectural designer—if for no other reason than to have guidelines for your contractor and subcontractors, most of whom will probably have had little or no experience with barns or barn house construction. Another important reason for using an architect is that professionals are kept updated on the latest state-of-the-art products in the marketplace. They also have had experience with a multitude of products—some of which they would recommend, others on which they would definitely turn thumbs down.

CHAPTER THREE

Buying Land

You're in luck if you happen to find the right barn in the right place on the right piece of property, or if—through foresight or inheritance—you already own the land on which you plan to build. If none of the above apply, here are some suggestions that could be helpful when you begin your search for land.

It's best to buy land direct from the seller. If you buy from a developer, you'll pay a good deal more—including what the developer paid for the property, whatever improvements have been made, and, naturally, a nice little profit for the developer's enterprise and imagination in seeing the potential of your particular piece of undeveloped land.

Improved building lots are the most expensive. The advantage here is that the lot usually has the basics—water, sewage, utilities, roads—already taken care of. The land is probably also cleared, although you may want to do a little more strategic clearing for a view, outdoor living space, or gardens. Just be sure that the lot has not already been cleared to the point of savagery. Some developers seem to think that trees are their worst enemies.

Large parcels of land usually come cheaper, proportionally, than small parcels. So if you see some nice acreage that is more than you need or want, you might consider buying it and later selling some off.

Don't pass up a nice piece of property just because it happens to have a house on it. If it is in a desirable area, you could, like Jill Butler (see page 117), sell off the house with a certain amount of land, keeping the part you want for yourself—assuming, of course, that you can swing the deal in the first place. Depending on the seller's needs, you might be able to work out a mutually advantageous arrangement such as making a down payment and paying the balance in installments. If the seller is eager, say, to retire and move to Florida or some other Sun Belt area, this arrangement could provide a nice little retirement income. Bear in mind, too, that banks are more willing to loan money on a house with land than on just land.

By all means take advantage of local real estate offices, and make your search with the assistance of a broker or agent who knows the territory. Also, scan the local newspapers for land offerings and keep an eye out for Land for Sale signs.

When you find property that interests you, walk over it with the broker or seller. You'll want to learn the boundaries of the acreage and also look for a prime building spot. High ground with a pleasant view is, of course, the most desirable. A slight rise overlooking open fields and meadows is about as much as any of us could ask for our barn house. A gentle slope could be just right to nudge in a bank barn house.

Wooded land can be inviting, but if you have to do much clearing, it will cost plenty to take down trees and pull stumps. Keep in mind that you'll need space not only for your barn house but also for a driveway and an entry road, if one is necessary. If the house is surrounded by trees, you could begin to feel, as the trees mature, that they are closing in on you. This happened to us once. The second summer we lived in our house was a very wet one, and the trees and shrubbery had achieved almost rain-forest proportions. If you went out in the yard and looked straight up, you could see a round blue bowl of sky; every other view was trees, trees, trees. The next summer, that property went for a fair, but not excessive, price to a couple who above everything wanted a woodland garden. A lucky break for us.

If, on the other hand, you have found a wonderful building site that happens to have a stand of trees blocking a potentially great view, you can have a professional tree company, doing a careful pruning job, carve out a view for you. (Environmentalists, don't wince; this pruning doesn't really hurt the trees and it's a lot better than cutting them down.)

As you continue to land-hunt, note outcroppings of rocks. Handsome and soul-satisfying as rocks are, such outcroppings could indicate ledge rock underneath. This can require expensive blasting when you're ready to excavate for the house's foundation. Ledge rock can also be a problem when you're ready to install your septic system.

You should also watch for wet spots or puddles of standing water after a recent rain, which can indicate poor drainage of subsoil. This, too, can complicate installation of a septic system and almost guarantees that you'll have problems keeping a basement dry.

If there is marshy or swampy land on the property, find out if the area is under *wetlands protection* regulations. If so, your barnyard may have to be sited a specified distance from the wetlands area. By no means plan to fill in any wetlands without first checking state regulations.

If you have doubts about the suitability of the land for any reason, have a civil engineer or a local architect walk the property with you. Also try to find out from your real estate broker and other local residents if any large-scale developments—state or private—are planned for the area.

Unless you're very close to a town center, there probably won't be a municipal sewage system, so you'll need a septic system to handle household waste. If you're a first-time homeowner, a septic system can be a mystery. It simply consists of an underground holding tank, where bacteria reduces much of the solid waste to liquid, and a leaching field or drywell, where the liquid is absorbed into the soil and eventually rendered harmless by the action of other bacteria. The holding tank must be pumped out by a professional tank-cleaning company every year or two, depending on how many people occupy the house and how much the system is used.

The only way to find out if a particular area is suitable for a septic system is to have a percolation, or "perc," test performed by a licensed septic system firm. A number of holes are drilled in a selected spot and are filled with water. How rapidly the water is absorbed into the soil is the key indicator to suitability. If one spot doesn't make it, they will usually try others. Once they find the right spot, they should be able to give you a reliable estimate of installation costs.

It is not uncommon to have trouble finding a suitable place for the septic system, especially on high, rocky ground. The Bloom barn house (see page 81) had multiple problems with septic installation, and we know of one couple who, because they had to bring in hundreds of yards of fill before their system would work, had to spend all the money they had allotted for their swimming pool—some $30,000. (Gulp.)

If you need a well, there's no point in expecting any sort of estimate—except, of course, how much it will be per drilled foot. The well driller doesn't have a firm idea of how far he is going to have to go down before finding an adequate flow of water. All you can do is pray that the drill hits a good gusher before it has to go to the ends of the earth. In the East, 200 to 400 feet is considered average, but it can be a lot more. In the West—parts of California, for instance—600 to 800 feet is not considered excessive. Around the country, costs can run from $5 to $12 or more per foot.

Before you get too involved, and definitely before you put down any money, be sure to check local *zoning ordinances*, which control the use of land as well as other physical characteristics. These ordinances are drawn up and enforced by a *Planning and Zoning Board*. If your proposed building site is a considerable distance from a main road, get estimates from a road-building or paving contractor on the cost to bring in a road or driveway. Also ask your local utility company what it will cost to bring in electricity. Sometimes the cost of these two items can take the bloom off of what seemed at first to be a bargain piece of land.

Finally, you want to make sure that the property you are interested in—and the surrounding areas—are zoned exclusively for residential use. Commercial or industrial enterprises later on would probably not be exactly what you had in mind for friendly neighbors. Zoning ordinances also stipulate the minimum lot size on which you can build, and the minimum distance a house—or other building—must be set back from the road and from the property lines. You may plan to sell off some of your property, now or in the future, or to renovate an old barn, only to find that certain zoning ordinances could prevent it.

In such a case, your next step would be to apply to the Planning and Zoning Board for a *variance*—an exception to the regulations. It will be granted if your request seems reasonable to the board or beneficial to the general neighborhood, or if you can prove hardship. If that fails, you could go to the *Zoning Board of Appeals* with your most persuasive arguments. If your appeal is denied, you must change your projected plan to conform to regulations, or forget the whole thing. You will be unable to get a building permit unless you can obtain a variance.

CHAPTER FOUR

How to Look
for a Barn

You no doubt already have a fairly definite idea of where you want to live, or where you'd like to have your vacation or weekend barn house, so it goes without saying that you'll start your barn scouting in and around that area. If you can make a leisurely survey, it's a lot more pleasant, of course, but not all of us have the time to do that. Here are a few pointers on how to get quicker results.

Keep an eye out for a barn that looks unused, perhaps surrounded by weeds and high grass. Make a note of exactly where the barn is—nearby landmarks and so on. If the barn has any distinguishing characteristics, make a rough sketch of it. When you find one or more that interest you, go to the Town Hall in the nearest town and find out if the barn you describe is in its territory. If it is, the tax assessor can give you the name of the owner and tell you how to contact him or her.

Visit the Town Hall

Even if you haven't turned up a barn, the Town Hall is well worth a visit. Ask around to find the best person to talk with about your barn quest. It may be the town clerk, a tax assessor, a building inspector, a zoning official, or the person in charge of road maintenance. Any of these people might have some leads. Try to arrange your visit when things don't look too busy.

Before you take your leave, ask where the Co-op Extension Service and the county agent's office are located. This service is administered by the U.S. Department of Agriculture and counsels farmers and others about all kinds of things related to the land, including crops, gardening, insect control, animal husbandry, and so on. The county agent might very well know of an available barn, if not in his territory, perhaps in an adjoining community.

Advertise

Put a Barn Wanted ad in the local paper and make the classified section of each issue your friend. You may see barns, barn frames, even old barn boards and barn flooring, advertised. Any of these are worth at least a phone call.

Get Help from Others

The more people you talk with, the better your chance of finding what you want. Local real estate brokers may have listings for farms or houses with barns, or may know of an available barn. If they see that you're a serious buyer, they will make an effort to track one down for you.

Architects, too, may know of barns—especially the younger architects, who are often great admirers of the way the old barns were built. They might even let you in on a special barn they already have an eye on—especially if there's a chance they might do the barn conversion.

Also check with the local fire department and the local lumberyard and hardware store.

A friendly waitress at a local coffee shop could be helpful; they overhear a lot of gossip and, who knows, some of it may have to do with an elderly party who wants to sell a barn and retire to Florida.

Local historical societies are good places to check. Some of these organizations make surveys of older structures in their areas and these can include antique barns. Also, they may have heard of someone who might be willing to sell a barn.

Widen Your Range

If you don't have to make a daily commute to a metropolitan area, or are planning a barn house for future retirement, you obviously have a much wider choice of places in which to barn-hunt. And, if you don't want to go completely rural, you might consider looking in or near a small town. You can often find some good buys near small towns or villages.

And remember, you are more apt to find a barn that goes with a house than just a barn. As we discussed in chapter 2, this decision has several advantages for you.

In a small town or village, check the older residential sections. Before the automobile took over, many houses in small towns—even rather grand houses owned by local bigwigs—had a barn on the property. A nearby barn was needed to stable the horse, store the hay, and house the family buggy. It's a long shot, but it is possible that there might be sufficient land involved so that the house and barn could be sold separately.

Move to ''Farm and Barn Bargain Country''

If you are a free spirit, able to roam, and can live any place you choose, look for some real bargains in the national real estate catalogs, such as Strouts or United National (see sources). When you write for a catalog, specify which sections of the country you are interested in.

You'll be pleasantly surprised at what you can get in some places for what is today a modest sum of money. One recent offering, for example, was for an Amish farm of 150 acres in New York State that included a 2,000-square-foot house—eight years old but with an unfinished second floor. There were two barns, one 32 by 50 feet and the other 40 by 46 feet, plus an 18-by-24-foot shop with a wood stove. And, oh yes, the property also included a strawberry patch and apple trees. Asking price: $46,000.

The newspaper published by the National Trust for Historic Preservation (see sources) runs ads for historic farms along with historic houses and other buildings, and is worth subscribing to. This organization, by the way, joined up with *Successful Farming* magazine in 1988, and sponsored the BARN AGAIN contest. The contest was designed to encourage farmers to rehabilitate their old barns to make them suitable for present-day farming methods, instead of tearing them down to be replaced by metal or concrete-block structures. Some of the entries in the contest were from people who had renovated their old barns for nonagricultural purposes such as offices, shops, and, in some instances, homes. Three of these contestants appear in this book (see the Petersons', Johnsons', and Dadeys' case histories).

Fine Homebuilding magazine (see sources) will sometimes run ads for old barns and barn frames in its classified section, and the *Newtown Bee*, a respected national newspaper for antiques dealers, also occasionally runs ads for antique barns and frames (see sources).

CHAPTER FIVE

How to Evaluate Your Barn House Before You Buy It

Whether you want to buy an old barn to renovate on its original site or one to disassemble and move, you must make sure that the wood frame is sound. So before you put down any money, the entire structure should be thoroughly inspected. You can do the preliminary inspections yourself, but a check by a professional restorationist is also in order.

Local Building Regulations

If you plan to renovate an existing barn where it presently stands, you first want to make sure that it can legally be transformed into a residence. Zoning and building regulations can prevent or at least delay a barn renovation. A particular barn, for example, may be too close to the road, or to the main house. It was no doubt built long before there were any zoning regulations that set minimum distances, so the old barn is allowed to remain as a "nonconforming" building as long as it is just a barn. But the only way to get a building permit to renovate it in its present location is to get a variance from the zoning board.

Arnold and Gerry Hanna (see page 63) had to get a variance because the barn they wanted to buy and renovate was only 30 feet from the road and local regulations required a 50-foot setback. They did get the variance but with one restriction: part of the barn had to be left in its original state.

Roads, Septic System, Water, and Utilities

Your second concern is to make sure that it is feasible to make these basic improvements. We discussed them in more detail in chapter 3 but mention them now to emphasize their importance.

Condition of the Barn

This is, of course, a major consideration. Often, you can tell if a wood barn is worth considering without even getting out of your car. If the roof is in bad shape—is missing shingles, has gaping holes, or is sagging badly—that barn is in trouble. If, in addition, the walls are aslant and the stone foundation is crumbling, drive on. It isn't worth further investigation. True, there might be some salvageable timbers, but that's another story we get to later.

Stone barns present a different picture. If the walls of a stone barn seem fairly intact, even if the roof looks pretty bad, it might be worth investigating. Much of the wood structure inside could well be usable.

Water is the chief enemy of all old barns, both wood and stone. Once the roof begins to go and rain and snow can enter, that barn is imperiled. If this is allowed to continue, rot and deterioration can be rapid.

Water from a leaky roof can damage the walls of a stone barn by seeping in through hairline cracks in the mortar between the stones. When the water freezes it expands and the cracks become wider. Unless the cracks are repaired, this freeze-thaw process is repeated year after year and eventually the wall is seriously damaged.

Moisture can reach wood not only through holes in the roof but through failing siding and through leaks around window and door frames. Rot is also commonly found in timbers such as sills, girders, and post ends in direct or close contact with masonry or the soil.

This wood rot is caused by an organism similar to the fungus that causes mildew. It thrives wherever moisture is present and can spread into wood like a cancer. Even if wood becomes dry at times, once attacked the rot continues, hence the term "dry rot." Sometimes wood rot appears on the surface as a powdery white blemish, sometimes as a discolored, darkish patch. Rot is not always visible to the eye.

Insects, too—carpenter ants, powder post beetles, and termites—can wreak havoc on wood frames. They often cause a lot of damage before they are detected, for they destroy wood on the inside and their presence is not generally visible. They do leave clues to their dirty work in other ways, though. Small, telltale piles of fine sawdust around timbers indicate the presence of carpenter ants. Holes, smaller than the head of a pin and often filled with fine sawdust, are a sign that powder post beetle grubs are at work. Termites can be detected by noting tiny earthen tunnels, called shelter tubes, on foundation walls. The termite workers create these tunnels so they can go from their underground nests to their woody feast without being exposed to the light.

To make a proper inspection, you will need some tools. Pick up a wire brush and a knife with a long, stiff blade at a hardware store. You probably already have a hammer and a flashlight. Wear work clothes with long trousers, a shirt with long sleeves, and heavy work shoes with thick soles. They will save you a lot of grief.

Use the knife blade to probe the wood for signs of rot and insect damage. If the blade goes in easily and breaks across the grain rather than producing long splinters, the wood is probably damaged. With the hammer, bang a section of timber. A soft rather than a solid sound means possible damage.

Use the wire brush to remove dirt and grime from timbers so you can see signs of decay and structural cracks. Don't be concerned about fine, hairline cracks, called checking, which occur normally when timbers season.

Some barn timbers, however, will show structural cracks—long, deep cracks that may run for several feet. These may occur when a timber is undersized for the span, or because an excess load was once imposed on it. In any event, the timber will have to be spliced with a sound timber in order to make it usable.

Begin your inspection at the bottom and work up. You cannot, of course, reach the higher timbers or the roof rafters without a ladder, but you will still be able to reach most of the critical areas, or at least enough to make a judgment. If the lower timbers are in bad shape, there's no point in going further, anyway.

Inspect any wood members that are in close or direct contact with the earth, or with masonry walls and foundations. Be especially careful to check the ends of timbers set into pockets in masonry. Where animals were once housed, decay in floor beams, floorboards, and ends of timbers is also highly likely. Manure and urine contribute much to wood rot.

Try to inspect each element in every area—foundation walls, girders and floor beams, sills, posts, all wood joints and joinery, and as many horizontal beams as you can reach.

Use your flashlight to check for water stains on the underside of roof boards. The water that caused these stains may have reached timbers set below the roof.

Keep a record of any elements that appear to be seriously damaged. If the majority of the timbers are in fairly good shape, then the barn is probably a good candidate for renovation.

Size of the Barn

Barns often run big—that's one of the things that make them so appealing. Renovation costs for a barn can run from $100 to $150 or more a square foot, depending on the degree of luxury you want. If you totally renovate two floors, for example, of a 40-by-60-square-foot barn, you're in for some pretty big bucks. Even at $100 a square foot, the 4,800 square feet of finished space will total $480,000. (Prices vary, of course, according to region.)

A big barn can provide space for an artist's studio, a gallery, or a photographic studio, in addition to ample living quarters. A big barn is also ideal for someone who operates a home business and requires office and storage space in addition to living quarters. Where zoning regulations permit, a large, attractively renovated barn can be an ideal bed-and-breakfast establishment or can include a rental apartment that can help pay off a mortgage.

If none of these possibilities is relevant and you still like a particular big barn, keep in mind that you don't have to renovate the whole thing. You can fix up just what you need and leave the rest unfinished. It can be divided from the living area by an insulated partition.

Get the Opinion of an Expert

It will now be worth it to get the opinion of an expert—an architect, a builder, a restorationist, or a timber framer who has had experience with antique barns and old houses. Ask the local historical society for names of suitable people and check the yellow pages under "Architectural" or "Building Restoration."

By the way, many restoration professionals keep an inventory of especially desirable antique barns. Sometimes these are barns that the restorationist has discovered over a period of time and has dismantled, coded, cleaned, and stored. In other cases, he has made an agreement with the owner of a barn to take it down and move it when the proper buyer is found.

CHAPTER SIX

Buying and Financing Your Barn House

That old chestnut *Caveat emptor* ("Let the buyer beware") is worth a thought as you set forth in search of your barn house. It isn't that the people you'll be dealing with—real estate brokers, bankers, builders, contractors, property owners—are out to take advantage of you; it's just that there are many complexities, leaving a lot of room for misunderstandings.

The best way to avoid any misunderstanding is to make no verbal agreements. This doesn't mean that a smile and a handshake aren't a nice way to start, but get everything in writing—spelled out in all possible detail. Read all agreements and contracts carefully—the fine print, too. If there are certain points to which you take exception, or that you don't understand, get them cleared up before you sign. If you are unsure of a meaning or find ambiguities, have an attorney check the agreement. (Actually, it's a good idea to do this anyway.) Choose an attorney who is familiar with real estate practices in the area where you are buying. A mortgage officer at a local bank or your real estate broker can give you names of suitable people. Attorneys' fees vary considerably, so ask about them in your first meeting.

We once paid an attorney $350 to handle a property closing. A neighbor of ours, at about the same time, paid another attorney $1,200 for almost the exact amount of work on a property closing very similar to ours in price and acreage. Both were professionals in the same town.

Contract for Sale

A contract for sale is the most important document in a real estate transaction. It not only spells out the details of a sale but is a binding legal agreement between buyer and seller. Unless you are willing to forfeit money, you can't change your mind once you've signed the contract.

The contract is usually a standard printed form with space left for contingency clauses by either buyer or seller. It will include a description of the property, sales price, method of payment, and any other pertinent details. It will state that a warranty deed must be delivered at the closing. This means that the seller will defend the deed against any and all claims, should it ever be questioned. The place, date, and time of closing will also be stated.

It's important that the contract include a clause to the effect that the sale is contingent on you, the buyer, being able to get a mortgage loan for a specified amount and at a specified rate of interest and term of mortgage. The clause should also state that if you are unable to get this loan by a specific date, you will not be subject to penalty (in other words, your down payment will be refunded to you).

If there is some question as to whether you might have to get a variance in order to use the property as planned, add a clause to that effect. The clause should include a time frame for applying to the planning and zoning board and getting a decision, and allow for the deal to be called off without penalty if you do not get the variance.

The contract for sale is usually filled out by the seller's broker. You may have spent considerable time with that broker and be on very friendly terms, but remember, when the broker hands you the contract, he or she represents the seller—not you. Read the contract carefully and ask your attorney to look it over, too. *Before you sign.* Also, make sure your attorney has a thorough understanding of how you plan to use the property.

Title Search

After you and the seller have signed the contract, a title search must be made to make sure the title to the property is clear. The title search is made by either your attorney, a title insurance company (if the lender requires you to take out title insurance), or an *escrow agent* (a neutral third party appointed by the seller's and buyer's attorneys).

The title search will provide a true description of the property and will certify that the seller has the exclusive right to sell. The search will also turn up any legal claims against the property. These are called encumbrances and may include one or more of the following three conditions.

Lien

This is placed against the property for unpaid taxes (local, state, and federal), for an unpaid mortgage or unpaid interest on a mortgage and other claims placed against the property. A *mechanic's lien* is placed against the property by a company, supplier, or workman who remains unpaid for work done on the property. Sometimes if there is a disagreement about the cost or quality of work, the company or individual who is owed money will slap a lien on the property to jar the homeowner into paying the bill. Regardless of the type of lien, all liens must be removed before the title is passed to the buyer.

Easement

An easement is the legal right granted to a third party for limited use of the property. A typical easement would be one granted to a power company to run and maintain power lines across the property. Easements go with the land. You just have to live with them.

Encroachment

This is a form of easement obtained because an owner was often careless in overseeing his property. If someone other than the legal owner has used any portion of the property for a specified number of years—ten years in many states—without objection or interference from the owner, that person then has what amounts to an easement and may continue use of the land with legal sanction. A common encroachment might be a road across a corner of the land to allow access to an adjoining property.

Assuming the title search doesn't turn up any unpleasant surprises, and that you have been able to get your loan from the bank or other lender, and that a variance—if you needed one—is approved, your next concern is closing costs. These can run into hundreds, perhaps thousands, of dollars.

Closing Costs

Within three days after your loan application has been approved, the bank is required by law to send you a *Truth in Lending* disclosure statement. This gives the details of your loan and lists all charges that must be paid before the bank will issue you the all-important check that will enable you to buy the property. Some typical bank charges are origination fees, discount points, credit report, appraisal fee, and, if you have a construction loan, an inspection fee. The disclosure statement may also include the cost of a title search, mortgage title insurance, and recording fee. Any other charges due at the closing should also be listed. These might include your share of real estate taxes prepaid by the seller and interest due on your loan from the day of the closing to the end of the month.

In some states—California, for one—the closing, title search, and other details are handled by an escrow agent. The escrow agent gets the deed from the seller, the money from the buyer, and, when all is in order, passes the deed to the buyer and the money to the seller. When it is all over, the escrow agent will send the buyer and the seller a statement listing their shares of the various costs involved.

The more common form of closing is a lot more personal and more satisfying. All the principal parties in the transaction meet in one of the lawyers' offices or the lender's office. The seller is there, along with the buyer, the two lawyers, the real estate agent or broker (this is when they get their commission), and a representative of the bank or lender handling the buyer's loan. Many of those in attendance have been through many closings together, so there is a good deal of good-natured talk as papers and checks are signed and passed around. In its own way, a closing such as this can be fun—fun for the seller because he or she walks away with a fat check; fun for the broker and the lawyers for they, too, get a check—now or in the near future. And it's fun for the buyer—who, although slimmer in pocketbook, is now the owner of the property.

Construction and Mortgage Loans

Whether you plan to buy and renovate an old barn or are going to build a new barn house, you will need a construction loan along with any mortgage money you require.

A construction loan is a relatively short-term loan—usually six months to a year—that is converted to a longer-term mortgage loan when the work is completed. The amount of money you can get on a construction loan depends on the value the bank puts on the to-be-completed project. The evaluation is based on your plans, specifications, realistic cost estimates, and on the fair market value of such a project at the time the transaction is negotiated.

You shouldn't plan on drawing on the loan any time you please. The bank will set up a payment schedule based on work actually completed. The bank officers will also inspect the work to make sure it is satisfactory before they hand over any money. Because interest rates on construction loans are higher than on long-term mortgage loans, it is to your advantage to get the work completed as quickly as possible so you can convert to the lower-interest mortgage loan.

Be sure that the construction loan gives you enough time to complete the house. Once the loan agreement has been written, it is hard to get it changed. Be realistic about the time you'll need. A barn house may run into special problems that make it more time-consuming to complete than a conventional house. If you are going to do all or most of the work yourself, you can try to get a construction loan for up to two years. You may not get it, but if you do, your incentive to hurry up and finish will be the high interest you're paying.

Don't expect the bank to put up all the money. You will be required to put some money up front yourself. This is your equity in the enterprise and is usually around 20 percent of the total projected cost. If you already own the land, the bank might consider this to be satisfactory equity, but don't count on it.

The bank officers will want plenty of detailed information before they'll give you the go-ahead, and they'll want it on paper. They will want to see floor plans for all levels of the projected building, plus elevations for all sides of the barn house—north, south, east, west. They'll want specifications for all basic materials and fixtures, heating, plumbing, types of windows, doors, insulation, furnace, and so on. They will want to see written estimates from contractors on materials they will supply and the costs of their labor. Your presentation should include cost estimates on every aspect of the work—septic system, driveway, foundation, framing, roofing, flooring, plumbing, wiring, heating. In addition, you or your contractor should prepare a schedule indicating the approximate time of completion for each of these projects.

The bank will also want to know your financial situation. This is the same information required for a conventional mortgage—total family income, whether dual or single, outstanding financial obligations, monthly payments for rent, installment purchases, credit cards, and so forth. If you pay alimony or child support, how much is it and for how long will you have to pay it? The bank may also want to see your federal tax returns for the past couple of years and know how much life insurance you carry.

If you don't have the time to locate a suitable bank, consider contacting a mortgage broker. You can get names from any real estate broker. Mortgage brokers specialize in obtaining suitable mortgages. They have contacts with many banks in the area—know their rates and the kinds of mortgages they do grant—so the broker can be helpful to you. And it is the bank, not you, who pays the broker.

Be forewarned that even after you have a weathertight shell erected, it still takes a tremendous amount of time to do the finish work on a house. Trying to do it just on weekends and during vacations can seem to take forever. Painting, flooring, tiling, window and door trim, and other jobs that you plan to do after you've moved in can seem like a snap—before you move in—but if you have a full-time job and you're trying to live your life as well, it can get a bit rough at times.

If you are planning to do all or most of the work yourself, you'll have to convince the bank that you have the time, energy, skills, and motivation to do the work and finish the job. Unless you are in one of the building trades, it can be hard to prove that you have the required skills. If you have attended building workshops and seminars or if you have attended a hands-on building school, they'll be impressed with your seriousness. Nancy and Gary Miers got a construction loan when they showed the bank the certificate they had received from The Shelter Institute in Bath, Maine, after having completed a fifteen-weekend building course.

If you have a relative or friend in one of the building trades who plans to work with you on your project, the bank will tend to look more favorably on your loan application. If you have a skilled hobby such as woodworking or cabinetmaking, they'd probably like that, too. If you have been a homeowner in the past, have some collateral, and can assure them that you can handle any cost overruns, you are proving yourself a responsible member of society in their eyes and, in the view of some ultraconservative banks, a person worthy of owing them money—even if you are building a barn house instead of a nice, conventional Cape or ranch house.

Shop Around for a Loan

It's a good idea to check with several banks before deciding which one to use. And you may well have to anyway before you find one that is interested in your project. Banks are a lot more skittish today than they were before the big S&L bust of 1989. They'd rather lend money on a conventional house built by a known contractor than on a barn house built by an unproved do-it-yourselfer. Nonetheless, since a lot more people are going in this direction, banks can and do make exceptions.

You, too, want to be selective. Compare interest rates not only on a construction loan but on the mortgage that will eventually replace it. Find out if you will have to pay *points* when your loan is converted to a mortgage. (A point is 1 percent of the total amount of a mortgage loan—on a $50,000 mortgage, a point equals $500—and is paid at the time the construction loan becomes your mortgage.) Also find out if there are other charges you'll have to pay at the time of conversion.

Once you get your construction loan, let the building and other trades people you'll be dealing with know about it. This will assure them that they'll be paid and will also alert them to the fact that the bank will be inspecting their work before giving a final okay for payment.

Keep in mind that a construction loan is a lien on your property. If you fail to keep up interest payments, don't complete the house in the agreed time, get behind in your real estate taxes, or, in case of some unfortunate happening such as a fire, if you don't have sufficient insurance to cover the value of the house, the bank can get plenty tough and take over the whole thing, lock, stock, and barrel.

When your barn house is completed, the construction loan is converted to a mortgage loan. This can be at a fixed rate or a variable rate. A fixed-rate loan ties you into a set interest rate for the life of the mortgage. If, at some future time, you feel you can do better and are willing to pay the various costs—sometimes even including more points—you can have the mortgage redrawn; or you can switch to another bank, where you'll have to start all over again. If you have an adjustable or variable-rate mortgage, the interest rate is reset every year and can go up or down depending on the primary interest rate. Be sure that there is a *cap*, which limits the increase in any given year to 1 or 2 percent; and, if possible, a *ceiling*, above which the interest rate cannot go no matter what happens.

Twenty
Case Histories

Eighteenth-century New England barn now used for large parties, guest quarters, and loft offices for the owner. Large windows were put in on east side, where old wagon doors once were, and a new door was added. Small window to right is original. Owners collect antique farm tools, which decorate the south wall, along with the old barn ladder. (Photo by H. and G. Orton-Jones.)

BARBARA AND EDMUND DELANEY

". . . the inside, we just kept simple."

———— ⌘ ————

Barbara and Edmund Delaney's barn "came with the house." So much so, in fact, that when they bought their eighteenth-century farmhouse in a small New England village some twenty-odd years ago, the real estate broker gave it a passing nod, and most assuredly did not use the tall, old cow-and-hay barn as a selling point. The Delaneys, too, busy renovating the house and getting settled, paid little attention to the barn, noting only that it was somewhat dilapidated.

One stormy day, a few months after they had moved in, they noticed that the northernmost wall of the barn appeared to be loose at the top corner and was moving back and forth in the wind. Investigation showed that squirrels had chewed through the wooden pegs joining the timbers at that corner. After having this repaired—it turned out the problem was not serious—closer inspection proved the barn to be in good condition, with the exception of floorboards in the lofts, which were rotted out (not surprisingly, because the most recent tenants had very obviously been chickens). The hand-hewn, chestnut timbers of the old 28-by-36-foot frame were sound, and, interestingly, a few of the timbers had ax marks quite different from those on the rest. The Delaneys surmised that these timbers had come from an earlier structure, and that the farmer, with true Yankee thriftiness, had salvaged and recycled them.

Why let all this wonderful space go to waste, Barbara and Edmund asked themselves. They loved the house but, as with most farmhouses of that period, the rooms were small. They decided to renovate the barn. They would use the large lofts on the second level as separate offices, one for each. Barbara had been managing editor of a well-known national antiques magazine and continued to contribute articles. She was also heavily involved in various historical and civic activities. Edmund, a practicing attorney in New York and author of several books, had become associated with a nearby law firm, but wanted an office at home for his writing. The space would be perfect.

Downstairs, they would use that portion of the barn that was open to the roof as an airy dining space when they wanted to entertain large

Italian chandelier hung from a roof rafter presides at dinner parties. Long picnic tables can seat up to twenty, but are often pressed into service for bounteous buffets for larger parties. Windows in rear were added. (Photo by H. and G. Orton-Jones.)

groups. The rest of the space on the first level they would use as a sitting room, furnished with antiques and French reproduction chairs and tables from Edmund's old apartment in the city. The main idea was to keep it simple and keep it "barny," rather than to do a lot of elaborate remodeling. After all, the house was where they lived—the barn would simply be an adjunct to that.

After replacing the loft floors, walls between all posts and other exposed timbers were insulated and drywalled. Drywall only was installed between the beams supporting the loft floors, giving the living room ceiling beneath a more finished appearance and helping to keep dust from drifting down from above. Only minimum insulation was used in the walls (this was before the energy shortage in the seventies), and therefore all timbers were exposed almost to their full depth. An open stairway was put into the new office spaces in the loft, replacing the old ladder that had once served as access.

Electric baseboard heat was installed, but is now used only when they are entertaining, since energy prices are far higher than they were when the barn was first renovated. For daily use, a wood stove—"Vermont

Chairs and tables in the French manner and European antiques are a pleasant and eclectic blend with the old timbers and the Vermont Castings wood stove. The dining space is beyond, screened by bamboo-stick porch blinds. (Photo by H. and G. Orton-Jones.)

Castings, engineered like a furnace"—keeps the place cozy, except in extremely cold weather, when it is backed up by kerosene heaters.

In 1980, a neighbor who was renovating his house removed a large, glassed-in porch, which the Delaneys decided would make a fine kitchen addition to their barn. They were right. It worked perfectly and, with a few adjustments, was attached to the rear of the barn. Plumbing was put in at the same time and a lavatory was installed. The barn could now serve as a comfortable guest house, along with its other useful functions. Partitions were put in only between the original barn and the "new" kitchen addition and lavatory. Otherwise, sliding bamboo shades and a small louvered panel behind the wood stove were used as room dividers between the dining and living room spaces. Both loft offices were left open to the dining area below, which can seat at least twenty people and is open to the roof peak.

The tongue-and-groove siding on the exterior was in good shape, as were the roof shingles, so no major repairs were needed. A large picture window was installed on the east side where the old wagon doors had once been, and a sixteen-pane window was put in above to bring in natural light to the office. On the west side, a row of sliding windows was added to light the other loft office.

The Delaney barn has become well known in the village and has been the scene of many celebrations, parties, and political and civic meetings. It's a fun place to visit—a unique combination of both simplicity and sophistication.

The 170-year-old Quackenbush barn as it was being dismantled by the New Jersey Barn Company for shipment to the O'Briens' property in Maryland, where it would be re-erected and made into a spectacular barn house. (Photo by the New Jersey Barn Company.)

GAIL AND JOHN O'BRIEN

". . . it was a real labor of love."

———⟨∞⟩———

"What you want is a barn," an architect friend told John O'Brien, who was living in Princeton, New Jersey, and had just described the kind of house he wanted to build on fifteen acres he had recently purchased on the Wye River in Queenstown, Maryland, on the eastern shore of Chesapeake Bay.

He hadn't seen any likely-looking barns when he and his fiancée, Gail, were scouting the area looking for property. John, a management consultant specializing in executive training, wondered where he could get a barn. "I'll find you one," replied his friend Harrison Fraker, now dean of architecture at the University of Minnesota.

Shortly afterward, Fraker introduced John to Alex Greenwood of the New Jersey Barn Company, also in Princeton. Greenwood, who specializes in the dismantling and re-erection of antique barns, was able to show John several. The one he finally selected had belonged to the Quackenbush family and was a partially disassembled three-bay, 40-by-50-foot post-and-beam barn built in 1824. It particularly appealed to him because of the

way the space was allocated, especially the 18-foot-wide threshing floor, which ran the width of the barn from front to back, and because it was a tall barn—plenty of space for a three-story conversion. The $55,000 price, which included trucking the dismantled frame to Maryland and re-erecting it on-site, was agreeable to John, so the deal was made.

Greenwood and his crew finished dismantling the barn; coded, cleaned, and fumigated the timbers; loaded the 542 pieces of history on a flatbed truck; and delivered the cargo to John's building site.

"We had a real old-fashioned barn raising," John says. "I invited a lot of friends over to help. We were all, including Alex and his partner, very serious about re-erecting this historic old frame, so we played classical music of around the period when the barn was built. And to keep it authentic and do it the way it was done in 1824, all the timbers for the first-floor bays were raised by hand. We only used a crane later, to raise the timbers for the upper portion of the barn."

Once the frame was up, John and Fraker were better able to plan how to utilize the space, especially the threshing floor running through the center, which John wanted to keep open to the rafters almost 40 feet above. The challenge was how to retain this superb space and keep it

(Left) Now the O'Brien barn, re-named "The Wye Barn" since it is on the Wye River in Queenstown, Maryland. Open house celebration is being held on the south deck, facing the river. Note the skylights added to roof, instead of adding more windows. Just glimpsed behind peak of roof is the wooden silo where a spiral stairway was installed, rather than break up the large expanse of space in the barn with conventional stairways. (Photo by the New Jersey Barn Company.) (Right) View from the third-level bridge gives some idea of the massive fireplace, which was built by a Philadelphia master mason from 54 tons of Pennsylvania native fieldstone, trucked to Maryland. Comfortable sofa and chairs add warmth to the austere elegance of chimney breast and antique timber frame in this 3,000-square-foot barn house. (Photo by the New Jersey Barn Company.)

open, intact, and uncluttered, while still incorporating in the plan the rooms John needed.

The solution was both practical and aesthetically appealing. Downstairs, the living room and dining room would be in the center space—18 feet wide and open to above. The main entry would also be there, and an entry hall. To the left of the center space would be the kitchen, a breakfast room, and a pantry. On the right, facing east, would be a sun room/family room, a lavatory, and a coat closet.

On the second floor, above the sun room, the master bedroom, dressing room, and bath would be built, the center space remaining open. On the opposite side, above the kitchen, would be another bedroom, dressing room, and bath. A bridge would span the center space, connecting the two sides.

On one side of the third level would be another bedroom and bath, and on the opposite side a study, both sides again connected by a bridge across. Obviously, the views down and up would be spectacular—and all of it framed by the massive posts and beams of the old Quackenbush barn.

The next thing that seemed obvious was that the second-story and third-story levels would have to be reached by a stairway of some sort, but

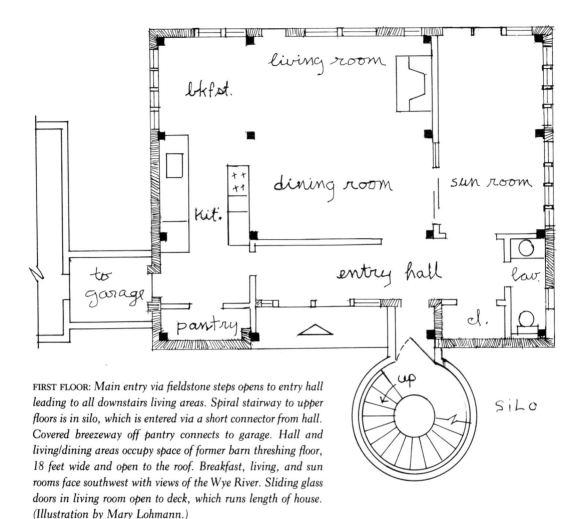

FIRST FLOOR: *Main entry via fieldstone steps opens to entry hall leading to all downstairs living areas. Spiral stairway to upper floors is in silo, which is entered via a short connector from hall. Covered breezeway off pantry connects to garage. Hall and living/dining areas occupy space of former barn threshing floor, 18 feet wide and open to the roof. Breakfast, living, and sun rooms face southwest with views of the Wye River. Sliding glass doors in living room open to deck, which runs length of house. (Illustration by Mary Lohmann.)*

the idea of putting conventional stairs in his barn house did not appeal to John. They would take up floor space he would rather leave open. So would a spiral stairway, although not as much. Then he was struck by a brilliant idea—what goes with a barn? Ah, ha, a silo! What about building a silo and putting spiral stairs inside with a landing on each level? The silo could be just outside, at the main entrance. But where to get someone to build a silo in the last quarter of the twentieth century?

Luck was with him. He was able to locate three Amish carpenters experienced in the craft of silo building. Using only hand tools, they built a 42-foot-high, 14-foot-diameter silo out of 1½-inch pine boards in seven

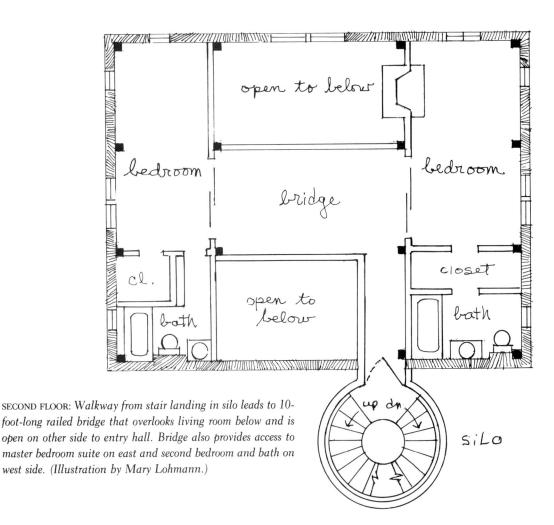

SECOND FLOOR: *Walkway from stair landing in silo leads to 10-foot-long railed bridge that overlooks living room below and is open on other side to entry hall. Bridge also provides access to master bedroom suite on east and second bedroom and bath on west side. (Illustration by Mary Lohmann.)*

hours. Seven *hours*, not seven *days*. The renovation of the barn would, of course, take a good deal more time than seven days—or weeks.

Luck was with John again when a builder friend from Philadelphia—"someone I knew and could trust to do the kind of custom work required on the house"—agreed to come down and bring his crew to work on the renovation. John, too, wanted to work on the project and also wanted to be around if problems arose and decisions had to be made. He had arranged to take three or four months off from his consulting business in Washington and now needed to find a place where he, the builder, and the crew could stay while the work was going on. He was able to rent a farmhouse about

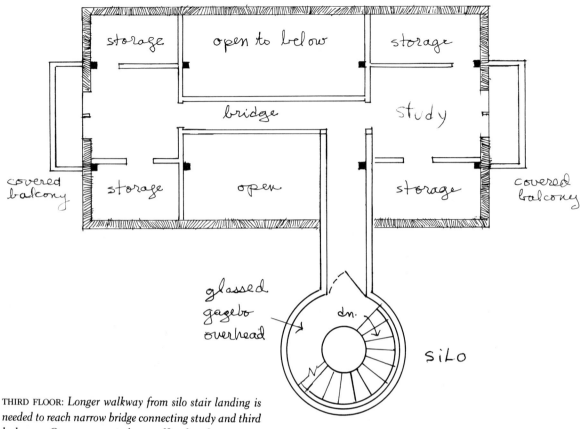

storage

open to below

storage

bridge

study

covered balcony

storage

open

storage

covered balcony

glassed gazebo overhead

dn.

SILO

THIRD FLOOR: *Longer walkway from silo stair landing is needed to reach narrow bridge connecting study and third bedroom. Owner uses study as office but has a more private office in the lighthouse gazebo at top of 42-foot-high silo. Gazebo has 360-degree view of countryside and is reached from third-floor silo stair landing. (Illustration by Mary Lohmann.)*

eight miles away and "hired a lady as a sort of 'housemother' to take care of us."

Work began in May of 1985 with a target date of October 12 to work toward. This was the day John and Gail were to be married—in the new barn house. "We really had to work," says John, "but it was a labor of love."

There was, of course, a great deal of work to be done. One out-of-the-ordinary undertaking was the building of a "connector" to join the silo to the house. This was accomplished by constructing a tall, narrow structure—"sort of like a milk carton," John says—which would run from the main-floor entryway to the third-floor level and provide sheltered access.

Doors would be installed at stair landings and walkways would be built to reach the bridges on each level. The connector was insulated, but the silo was not. Asked whether it didn't get pretty cold in winter, he said that it did, but "you're either running up or down the stairs, so it really doesn't bother you."

The main house was insulated and made snug with stress-skin panels applied to walls and the roof. There are several large expanses of glass on the south side to obtain optimum heat gain in winter. Skylights are also set in the roof on that side for heat gain and to add natural light.

One job the "farmhouse crew" didn't tackle was building the fireplace and the three-flue chimney that runs straight up from the living room, reaching skyward past both second- and third-story bridges. Built of select Pennsylvania fieldstone by a Philadelphia stone mason, this massive structure perfectly complements the heavy structural timbers that define the entire space. So do the floors of 2½-inch-thick oak boards rejuvenated from old barn flooring.

By the day of the wedding, the renovation of the barn was completed— all 3,400 square feet. But just barely. "The morning of the wedding," John says, "we were still hauling remnants left over from carpeting the bedroom floors."

Today, in the late summer of 1990, the barn house is a lived-in and loved home for Gail and John O'Brien. The silo is now topped with a lighthouse gazebo, reached by a ladder from the top stair landing. While John uses the study on the third floor as one office, he has chosen this space as a very private office. When he looks up from his desk, he has a 360-degree view of the countryside and the Wye River.

Inside the house, the view is also spectacular. The total effect of the soaring spaces, coupled with the spare elegance of the old barn frame and the lavish display of fine masonry in the fieldstone chimney breast is, to say the least, impressive. And, in the old sense of the word, before it became an overused adjective for almost everything—awesome.

Looking from living room to dining space and beyond to kitchen. Glass doors lead to deck on south side. Plywood subflooring will be covered with ash or oak. Biscuit-colored ceramic tile will be used for kitchen flooring. (Photo by Tom Hopkins.)

SISSY AND JIM DISERIO

". . . a pretty tired barn."

———————⊷⊶———————

In July 1985, Sissy and Jim Diserio, disenchanted with suburban living, bought a 200-year-old stone bank barn in Newtown Square, Pennsylvania. The barn was, as Jim put it, "pretty tired." The roof was practically nonexistent, the south wall—the only wood frame side—was leaning dangerously, and water had even seeped into the 20-inch fieldstone walls, damaging the mortar that bonded the stones together. The leaking roof had caused extensive rot in the main-floor planking as well as in the old log floor beams and many of the horizontal timbers.

Despite the condition of the barn, the Diserios saw promise in it and bought it that same month for $60,000. They had sold their suburban house and used some of the money to buy the barn.

Sissy had fallen in love with the property—the once-handsome old barn, inscribed "1791" on an outside stone, was surrounded by four acres of fields and meadowland—plenty of space for kids, gardens, and animals. Jim was fascinated by the historic barns of Pennsylvania and had read many old books about them. This barn, while large by some standards, was 36½ feet by 46½ feet—smaller than many similar stone barns in the region; but Jim figured that by adding a second floor (the lofts were long gone) the family could have a total living space of 2,800 square feet—more than their previous house and ample for their present needs.

Jim works for a firm that installs and replaces chalkboards, and he had also built their previous house, so he felt confident that with Sissy's two brothers he could handle the barn renovation. They would live with Sissy's mother until things were far enough along so that they could move in, and they'd do the remaining work after that, as time allowed.

The first step was to draw up the plans. The layout was to be simple; living space would be arranged around existing posts and beams, leaving as many of the old timbers exposed as possible, with a goal of achieving an airy, open feeling. They wanted to arrange the rooms to take advantage of existing windows, because Jim was afraid that the old stone walls would be seriously undermined if openings had to be made for additional windows and doors. The front entrance, for example, was to be set into the same

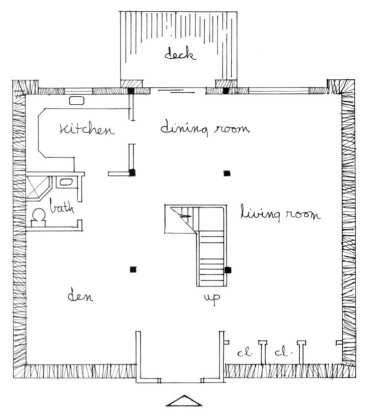

FIRST FLOOR: *New front door was set into space where old barn doors once opened onto former threshing floor. Now used as a 12½-foot-wide center hall running entire width of barn with stairs to second floor and dining area at end. Living room, 36½ feet long, is at right. (Illustration by Mary Lohmann.)*

opening on the roadside where the old wagons used to be driven in to what was once the threshing and granary floor. The old wooden barn doors would flank the new door.

Since there were no lofts left in the old structure, a whole new second floor would have to be built to provide space for a master bedroom and bath. Two other bedrooms would be separated from the master suite by a large family bathroom and a wide hall where the stair landing would be. The hall was to have a balustrade at the south end and overlook the open dining area below.

The plan was to finance the renovation out of income, because "no one would give us a mortgage on a place in the condition this one was in." They didn't even bother to shop for a construction loan because they had absolutely no idea of how long it would take them to complete the renovation.

There was a lot of hard work ahead. The Diserios, with some help from family members, worked evenings, weekends, and vacations. Sissy

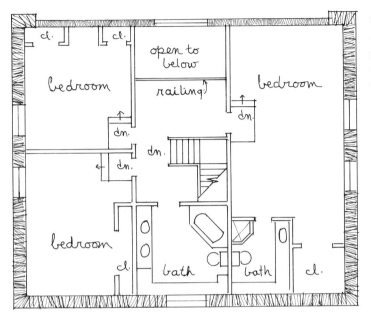

SECOND FLOOR: *Old hay-and-grain loft timbers were rotted out, so a complete second floor was built. Balcony at stair landing looks down on dining area. (Illustration by Mary Lohmann.)*

had a part-time job, but worked on the house during the day whenever she could. Their son Dustin, at age six, did what he could fetching and carrying (Jim Jr. was only three). One of the first things to be done was to demolish and rebuild the wood frame south wall. A new roof had to be put on and a second floor built, practically from scratch. Jim also built a complete basement on the grade level where the animals had once been housed. He used this as his workshop and also as a place to store building materials.

They decided to insulate large areas of the stone walls on the inside so that the beautiful stonework on the exterior could be left exposed. But before the walls could be insulated, they had to be repointed with fresh mortar. They were made watertight with a coat of "parge"—a type of mortar. A 2-by-6 stud wall was then set just far enough away from the stone so that it could be made plumb. Insulation and a vapor barrier was applied, and then the inside face of the stud frame was covered with drywall and painted.

According to Jim, one of the most difficult jobs of the entire renovation was rebuilding the rotted-out first floor. All the old planking had to be removed, along with 80 percent of the old log floor beams. But before any of this could be done, the vertical posts resting on the floor had to be supported with jacks and held in place with braces.

Another tough job was the roof. Although the purlins were in good shape, the roof boards and the rafters had been damaged by rot. The roof had to be repaired one small area at a time so that water would not reach the newly completed second floor. Jim and Sissy would rip off the old shingles and rotted cedar roof boards, then repair or replace rafters, install 1-by-3 roof boards, then put on the new cedar shingles. It was difficult and time-consuming work but the only way to properly redo the roof.

Local codes required that plumbing and wiring be done by licensed mechanics, so they contracted out this work, as well as installation of the baseboard circulating-hot-water heating system.

When we visited Jim and Sissy in the spring of 1990, the renovation was completed except for the finish flooring and some interior trim work. They had built a large deck on the south side overlooking a lovely meadow. Glass doors leading from the dining area to the deck were topped by a large arched expanse of glass. New, wood-framed windows set a few feet from the doors brought in more natural light to the whole living/dining area, as did several windows on the south wall of the kitchen. Walls had been painted antique white, nicely setting off the exposed timbers—some old and some new, but all looking the same, as the new timbers had been treated to look old.

When Tom Hopkins, our photographer, visited a few weeks later, Jim had done the trim, and they were about to cover the now well-worn plywood subflooring with finish flooring of oak or ash.

GERRY AND ARNOLD HANNA

"An 1810 cow-and-hay barn . . ."

————————◦∞◦————————

When their son left for college in 1983, the Hannas decided to sell their ranch house and either buy or build something smaller and, as Gerry says, "a lot different from the ranch house."

While scouting the territory around where they lived in eastern Connecticut, Gerry, who teaches school in the area, happened to run across an old barn for sale in Columbia, not far from their old place. A cow-and-hay barn built in 1810, it was on a 2½-acre lot, and although close to the road, overlooked a lovely meadow on the south side. It was on the market for $35,000.

At first, Arnold, an area manager for the Southern New England Telephone Company, was not too enthusiastic about the idea of buying and fixing up an old barn, but he did ask an architect friend, Bob Gantner of Willimantic, to take a look at it. Gantner and Arnold spent a whole day going over the structure, concluding that it was essentially sound, with no rot in the timbers. Another concern was the condition of the old stone foundation. If it had to be replaced, there would be the considerable expense of jacking up the barn and rebuilding the stone walls or replacing the stones with poured concrete. Arnold asked the local building inspector to come over to examine the foundation, which, happily, was found to be in good shape. "This barn has been resting on those walls for nearly two hundred years. No reason why it shouldn't rest on 'em for another two hundred," the inspector told him.

The Hannas did find out, however, that in order to make the barn into a residence they would have to get a variance. Local ordinances required that a dwelling be set back fifty feet from the road, whereas the barn was only thirty feet back. In order to show the zoning board what the barn would look like from the road, after renovations, some preliminary drawings were made by the architect, showing that major changes would not be evident on the roadside and that the structure would still essentially look like a barn on that side.

The variance was granted, but with the stipulation that "some of the space be left unfinished." The entire barn could not be used as a residence.

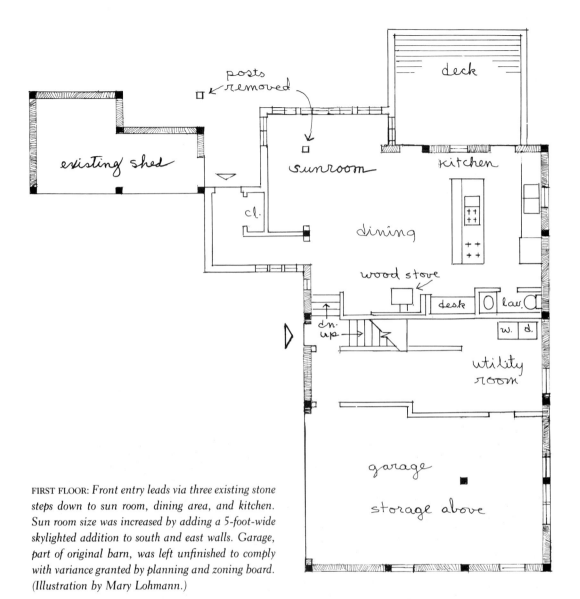

posts removed

deck

existing shed

sunroom

kitchen

cl.

dining

wood stove

desk

lav.

w. d.

utility room

dn. up

garage

storage above

FIRST FLOOR: *Front entry leads via three existing stone steps down to sun room, dining area, and kitchen. Sun room size was increased by adding a 5-foot-wide skylighted addition to south and east walls. Garage, part of original barn, was left unfinished to comply with variance granted by planning and zoning board. (Illustration by Mary Lohmann.)*

This was nicely solved by using the extra space for a garage on the first level and a large storage area on the second level.

With this major hurdle overcome, the sale finally went through and the Hannas started working on the plans in earnest. Arnold says admiringly that Bob Gantner and Gerry "put their heads together and with a lot of imagination and foresight" came up with a plan that suited everyone. "Lots

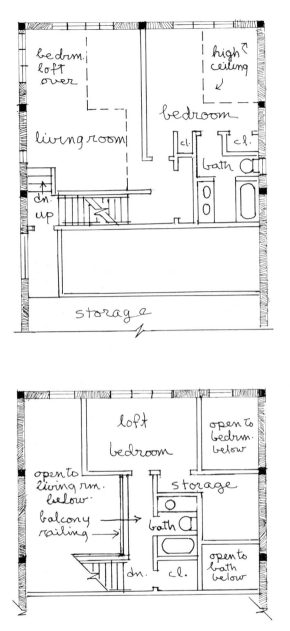

SECOND FLOOR: *Skylights set into roof bring light to living room and master bedroom, which has double-height ceiling. (Illustration by Mary Lohmann.)*

THIRD FLOOR: *Balcony providing access to loft bedroom and bath overlooks living room. (Illustration by Mary Lohmann.)*

of glass on the south side for Arnold" and "lots of wide-open space" for Gerry.

In order to comply with the terms of the variance, which allowed them to renovate only a 24-by-30-foot portion of the barn, the entry hall and an addition for a sun room on the ground level were added on the east side, away from the road. The two upper levels were to be a living room and bedrooms, with the living room ceiling open to the roof rafters.

Plans and specifications were given out to three contractors for bids. The low bidder was Northern Builders. While not experienced in barn renovations, the company had just taken on an experienced restorationist— Mike Barasso—so even though the $100,000 bid was somewhat more than the Hannas had planned to spend, they decided to go ahead with that offer.

Renovation work included breaking up the old concrete floor on the ground level and replacing it with new concrete, also building the sun room addition and insulating the outside walls. Arnold took on the miserable job of removing the years of accumulated dust and grime from all the timbers and from the underside of the roof. Wearing a hard hat, a ski mask, and goggles, he spent many jolly hours wire-brushing posts, beams, and rafters.

Insulation of the outside walls was done by installing 2-by-6 studding between the old timber frame floor, then setting fiberglass panels between the studs. Stairs from the first floor to the second and third floors had to be built; room partitions framed; and the usual heating, plumbing, and wiring installed. Arnold did all the wiring; plumbing and heating were contracted out.

In order to leave the newly clean and age-burnished roof rafters exposed—they can be seen from all levels of the house—the architect specified that the old roof be left in place, including the old shingles. A new roof was to be installed over the old with insulation applied between the old and new shingles. A "roof over a roof," in Gerry's words. This was accomplished by setting 2-by-10 rafters on top of the old shingles, applying insulation between, then adding plywood sheathing and, finally, the new shingles. To bring light into the living room and surrounding areas, including stairwells and landings, three skylights were installed side by side in the east roof over the living room. Two skylights were installed on the west side, over the master bedroom. Two paddle-blade fans were also installed high in the double-height ceilings so that air circulation in summer and in winter could be controlled. Heating is baseboard hot water, and with the fans circulating heated air throughout the house during the winter months, the Hannas' yearly heating bill is less than $800.

Because of the 2-by-6 studding on the exterior walls, the drywall on the interior had to be cut to fit against the sides of the posts, which the

Hannas wanted to leave exposed. Drywall applicators approached to do the job were reluctant because it would take too much time to cut and fit each drywall panel. The firm they finally found, however, did a first-class job. They even applied strips of masking tape to the sides of each post, so that the cut edges of the drywall would not leave chalk dust on the wood.

Once the drywall was in and painted a warm off-white, Gerry added a line of stencilling high on the walls of the living room and in the master bedroom on the third floor. An avid collector of antiques, she has used mellow old pine chests, painted bird decoys, and other American country collectibles in strategic areas throughout the house, which gives the proper "barny" atmosphere to a very successful renovation.

The worst part of the entire project, Arnold reports, was the drilling of the well. They had budgeted for a well about 200 feet deep, but when the well driller had to go down 800 feet before an adequate supply of water was found, the $5-a-foot charge, plus the cost of a heavy-duty pump, knocked a big hole in their "contingency" budget. Most other costs came in pretty much as projected.

Renovation on the barn started in January of 1986 and was completed by June—not a bad record considering that so much of the work had to be done during a New England winter. Total cost, including barn, land, and renovation work, came to about $180,000. Again, not bad at all, considering that the real estate market and costs of labor were approaching their peak just about then.

The Hannas are delighted with their barn house—both for the manner in which it was laid out (Arnold gives Gerry most of the credit for design and layout) and the workmanship that went into the renovations. In fact, their barn house has become a real showcase for Mike Barasso's talents. Mike had done some restoration work before, but had never worked on a barn. A "perfectionist" and "ingenious" in all kinds of ways, according to the Hannas, he has gotten some very nice jobs from people who have visited the Hanna house and admired his work.

*Set on the edge of a field, this barn house, with its clean
lines, is reminiscent of an old barn that has been renovated.
This one, however, is a new barn house built from a complete
package kit from Yankee Barn Homes. (Photo by Suki
Coughlin/Stylist Paula McFarland.)*

PAULA LANDESMANN

"I can't speak highly enough of them."

———⟨∞⟩———

When Paula Landesmann decided to build a vacation house—a retreat from her home in Manhattan—she began looking for a suitable piece of land on which to build. She wanted to be away from the city, but not so far away that she couldn't go up on weekends. In the spring of 1987, she found just what she was looking for—fifteen acres in Columbia County, New York, and only about a two-hour drive from New York City. The land had once been part of a large farm and included an ideal site for her projected house—a hilltop on the edge of a field. She bought the acreage for $70,000. Now all she needed was the house. She knew what she wanted but she didn't want to get too involved in the construction process.

Since Paula seemed a perfect candidate for a precut, manufactured house, the real estate broker who handled the property sale gave her some literature on a number of firms offering different types of packaged houses.

Paula was particularly impressed with the post-and-beam designs offered by Yankee Barn Homes in Grantham, New Hampshire. The two-story-high living room appealed to her, as did the "barn" look, which seemed just right for her acreage. The house would be delivered as a completed package, and since all building components were precut, it could be assembled and finished in short order—exactly what she had hoped for.

She got in touch with the Yankee Barn people and shortly afterward drove to New Hampshire, where she met with the principals and with the design staff. She was shown different types of houses and could see firsthand how they were built and the quality of the workmanship. Yankee Barn has been producing complete kits since 1968, and has been a major influence in the popularizing of post-and-beam, double-height-ceiling homes. Their first basic model—the Mark I—was the one that seemed to offer many of the things Paula Landesmann was looking for, and she was assured that the design staff could make any adjustments or changes that she felt necessary.

The fireplace is the focal point in the living and dining area. A tall brick chimney complements timbers that frame the double-height living room. Antique afghan on sofa adds multicolored old-time charm. (Photo by Suki Coughlin/Stylist Paula McFarland.)

Among her major requirements, she told the designers, were a large, airy living room with a fireplace; a dining area; and a compact kitchen. She also wanted a master bedroom and bath downstairs. On the upper level, she needed two bedrooms and a bath for guests and visiting grandchildren. She didn't want a large house, but it shouldn't seem cramped.

After the plans were customized to her requirements and approved, a foundation plan was worked up. A copy was given to Paula so that work

Sliding doors in center of large glassed expanse on south side lead to deck that runs length of barn house and to perennial gardens planted by owner since photographs were taken. Some of these windows can be opened, but entire top expanse is stationary. Balcony at head of stairs overlooks living room and leads to two bedrooms and a bath on second floor. (Photo by Suki Coughlin/Stylist Paula McFarland.)

on the site could begin and the foundations be finished and ready when the house was delivered.

Back in Columbia County, she lined up Larry Cavagnaro of Old Chatham, a general contractor who would oversee construction and handle installation of heating, plumbing, and wiring, the only things not included

FIRST FLOOR: *Planned as a comfortable, convenient weekend and summer place, this house has its master bedroom and bath on the first floor—a prime requirement, since the owner did not wish to climb stairs. The centrally located fireplace serves both dining and living areas. Windows and sliding glass doors are placed to take advantage of views of surrounding fields. (Illustration by Mary Lohmann.)*

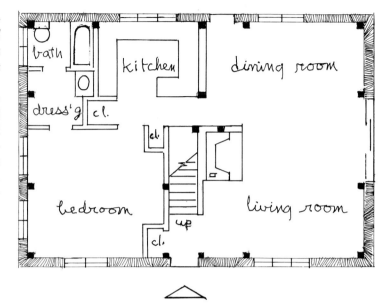

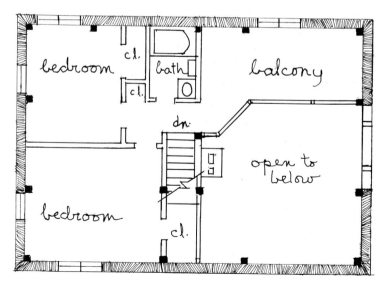

SECOND FLOOR: *Bath is positioned to be convenient to both bedrooms and to living area stairs. Railed balcony overlooks living room. (Illustration by Mary Lohmann.)*

in the package. The kit contained everything else—from the framing timbers to windows, doors, and even interior trim. All elements were precisely precut with clearly drafted blueprints indicating just where everything was to be. The package arrived in October and the house was completed in January. A rainy fall and winter slowed things down a bit, so it took longer to finish than anticipated. "If it had not rained all the time," Paula says, "my house would have been finished in four months, not the five it actually took."

The rain and the fact that the well driller had to go down farther than the budget allowed were the only negative factors in the whole experience, Paula feels. "They had to go down 400 feet to get water. That well ended up costing me $5,000," she laments.

The total cost of this comfortable and attractive barn house was $215,000. The Yankee Barn package was $70,000; the plumbing, heating, electrical work, septic system, and contractor supervision cost another $70,000; and there was the initial $70,000 for the land.

Paula Landesmann remains very much impressed with the whole Yankee Barn experience. "I can't speak highly enough of them," she says. They told her in advance what the house, customized to her needs, would cost, and according to her, "it turned out to be almost exactly that amount." In an era when cost overruns are the order of the day, this was indeed unusual.

The first of five barns arrived on the site in October 1977. The Dadeys paid $100 for the barn and another $700 to have it moved to their land in Marquette, Nebraska. (Photo by Ed Dadey.)

JANE AND ED DADEY

"Our project is successful, but its completion is still a decade away."

◆

The studio/residence assembled by Jane and Ed Dadey from five old barns moved from abandoned farmsteads to their five acres in Marquette, Nebraska, is known locally as the "Marquette Mega-Mall."

Nestled into the flat Nebraska farmland, the Mega-Mall includes 12,000 square feet of floor space, a four-story 65-foot cupola complete with its own elevator, and a two-story passive solar greenhouse.

Both Jane and Ed are artists engaged in a variety of creative activities—woodworking, metalwork, ceramics, photography, computer graphics, original design quilts and baskets, and one-of-a-kind avant-garde furniture. They realized several years ago that old barns would be a satisfying and inexpensive way to get the tremendous amount of space they needed for their many activities. "Pragmatically, we were looking for a large space at low cost," Ed says. "But, intellectually, we wanted a future for doomed buildings that were sociologically important, and which, modified for other purposes would remain to enrich the community."

The Dadeys' project began in 1976 when they started moving one barn a year. They paid $100 for their first barn—a combination post-and-beam and stud construction—and $700 to have it moved by a professional house mover. They paid another $100 for one other barn, but they got the rest, which were all stud construction, for free. The owners had just wanted to get them off their property. One of the free barns was an enormous hay, cow, and calf barn, 50 feet by 50 feet. The barns ranged from about sixty to eighty years old, the oldest having been built around 1910. Ed Dadey says old barns like these are just not available today. They have been either demolished or converted to residential or commercial enterprises. While the Dadeys' complex is still in farm country, bedroom communities—from which people commute to Lincoln, Nebraska's capital, or to Grand Island, the nearest town of any size—are coming closer all the time.

The barn that is slated to become their permanent residence is set somewhat apart from the others. (As of July 1990, they were still living in

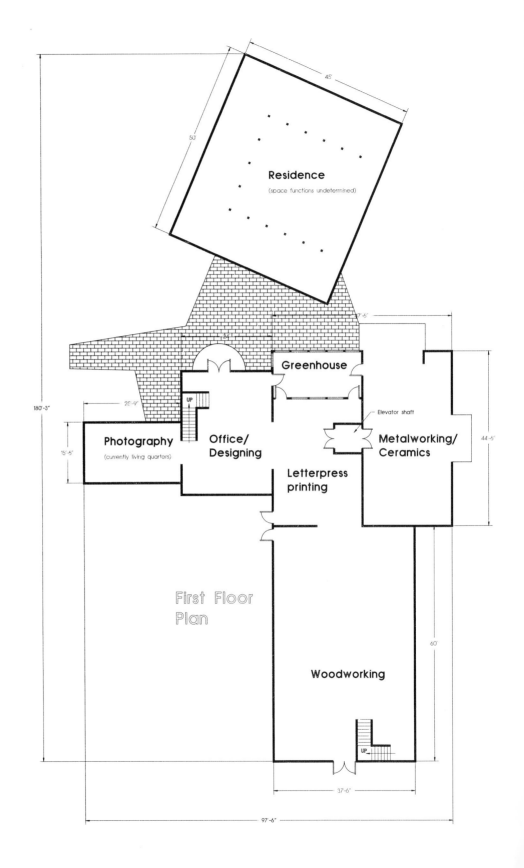

Residence
(space functions undetermined)

45'

50'

180'-3"

Greenhouse

7'-6"

34'

25'-9"

UP

Photography
(currently living quarters)

**Office/
Designing**

Elevator shaft

**Metalworking/
Ceramics**

15'-6"

44'-6"

**Letterpress
printing**

First Floor
Plan

60'

Woodworking

UP

37'-6"

97'-6"

Studio/Home
of
Ed & Jane Dadey

Diagrammatic drawing produced by Ed Dadey shows how four old barns were assembled to form a huge studio/workshop and a fifth barn was set apart from the others for a future residence. (Illustration by Ed Dadey.)

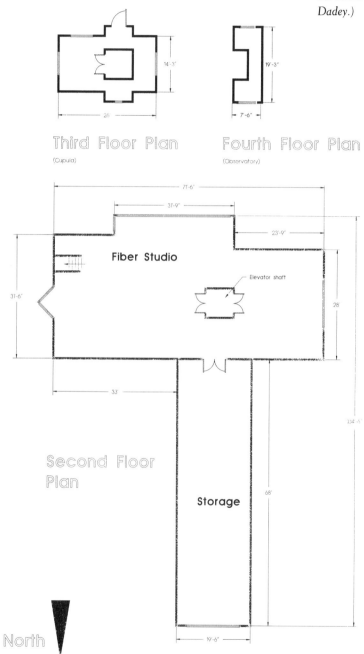

Third Floor Plan
(Cupola)

Fourth Floor Plan
(Observatory)

14'-3"

26

19'-3"

7'-6"

Second Floor Plan

Fiber Studio

Elevator shaft

31'-6"

71'-6"

31'-9"

23'-9"

28'

104'-6"

33'

68'

Storage

19'-6"

North

temporary quarters in the photography studio.) The remaining 80 percent of the total space is devoted to the studio work areas.

Special places in the complex have been designated "getaway" spots for those times when the Dadeys have had enough for a while. The Time Out Room, a space about 24 feet by 13 feet, is in the cupola, and at the very top of that tall structure is a smaller space, the Far Out Room, where a thirty- to forty-mile view of the countryside can be seen from every compass point.

Jane and Ed are doing all the design and construction work on their vast project themselves. This includes all carpentry, the taking down of walls, and building the towering cupola—which now includes a passenger elevator they salvaged from a local hospital that was being demolished. All they had to do was haul it to their place. (And, we add, have the ingenuity, talent, and know-how to install it and get it running.)

Salvaged materials play a big part in the Dadeys' endeavor, and since

they are using the pay-as-you-build method of financing, they keep a sharp lookout for buildings that are being razed or are about to be demolished. Every doomed building is worth checking for equipment or other material that might be useful.

Because they have been able to use so much salvage, and have done most of the work themselves—including heating, wiring, and plumbing—the project so far has cost only around $7,000. Most of that, according to Ed, went into moving the barns, installing the foundations, and paying for roofing shingles.

The heating system is an interesting industrial-type radiant heat that is generated by a gas-fired burner. A vacuum pump in the attic pulls the heat from the burner through heavy 2½-inch metal pipes that are suspended from the ceiling and which radiate heat downward.

When we last spoke to the Dadeys, in July 1990, they had not as yet gotten around to completing their "residence." They've also added one more activity to their busy lives—organic farming—on part of a recently inherited forty acres, which now brings their total acreage up to forty-five. So far, says Ed, in trying to avoid using pesticides, their biggest crop is "weeds in a row." But it does take time, he says, to build up the soil so that organic farming will succeed. And indeed, patience and perseverance appear to be among their major characteristics. With his dry, tongue-in-cheek humor, Ed says philosophically, "Similar to Rome, this project has not been appropriated full funding and given operational status in one day."

After the barns were assembled on new foundations, walls between were removed so interior traffic patterns could be planned. On the third floor of the cupola is the Time-Out Room—a relaxing 24-by-13-foot space. A much smaller Far Out Room on the fourth level offers 30-to-40-mile views of Nebraska countryside. (Photo by Ed Dadey.)

Cool, contemporary look of furnishings is in crisp contrast to warmth of exposed timbers in ceiling and polished wood floor. Book-lined wall and baby grand piano are invitations to pleasant, relaxed living in the delightful room. (Photo by Tom Hopkins.)

ELIZABETH GWILLIM AND LARY BLOOM

"There were surprises everywhere, most of them nice ones. . . ."

———⦿———

Elizabeth Gwillim's and Lary Bloom's decision to build a new barn house was not their first idea. Their first idea, once the three daughters they had between them were in various stages of independence, was to escape the suburbs for the country—or at least a small town.

Having always admired Connecticut Valley towns, they began their real estate survey a few miles south of Hartford. When they found nothing suitable, they expanded their search and headed farther downriver until they realized that they were only a few miles from Chester, a little town that they had always thought to be the prettiest in Connecticut. Chester is about equidistant from Hartford, where Lary, an editor/writer, works, and the shoreline town where Elizabeth works in public relations. Yet the search in Chester was fruitless, too.

It was then that the idea struck to buy some land in Chester and build a new house. They were living in a three-year-old house with Victorian touches, designed and built by architect Jeffrey Linfert, but they weren't really sure what style house they now wanted.

Linfert had recently built for himself a barn house in a country setting—an intricate and beautiful design. Elizabeth and Lary were intrigued by the open feeling of the house and also admired the post-and-beam construction. It seemed simple, yet offered surprises around every corner. The floor plan was highly creative, particularly the half-level space between floors, which appealed to them very much. They decided to ask Linfert to design a barn house for them on the land they had found in Chester—part of a former granite quarry, with wonderful outcroppings of rocks. The site was high on a hill with a marvelous view of the Connecticut River.

They also decided to use the post-and-beam timber frame package that had supplied the basic materials for Linfert's house: Habitat/American Barn. The firm would do the same for them, custom-cutting to their order all the basics needed for their barn house. The owners and architect worked for three months on the plans, modifying here and there, and eventually

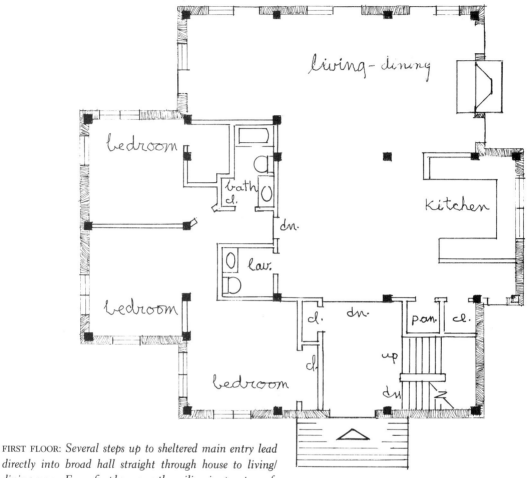

FIRST FLOOR: *Several steps up to sheltered main entry lead directly into broad hall straight through house to living/dining room. From fireplace area the ceiling is open to roof. Open kitchen is on right. On left, off hall, a step down leads to three bedrooms, bath, and lavatory. (Illustration by Mary Lohmann.)*

included Steve Worth, a representative of the company, in their planning discussions.

Linfert's design resolved two of the couple's main concerns: the wish to feature the outstanding view; and the desire to set off an area as the kids' wing—one that could be closed off when the young people were not around, which would probably be much of the time.

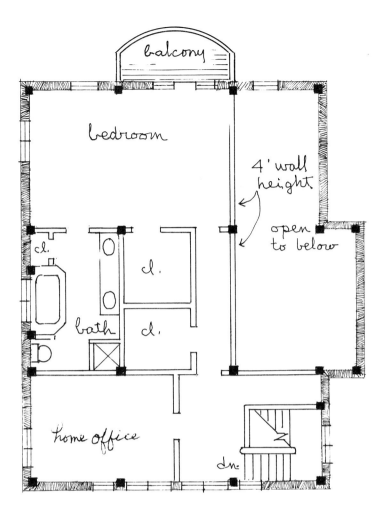

SECOND FLOOR: *Stairs lead to wide landing, then up to railed balcony overlooking kitchen, which provides bird's-eye view of what's cooking for dinner. Walk-in closets can be reached from bedroom or hall. Location of home office next to stairs allows visitors to office to come and go without disturbing household. (Illustration by Mary Lohmann.)*

Once the final plans were set, Steve Worth arranged for the barn package, the basic shell of the house, to be cut to order. The package would include posts and beams, decking, roofing materials, siding, windows and doors, and all other components required for a complete, insulated, weathertight shell. The owners were responsible for foundation and site preparation, erection of the package, all mechanical work and appliances, cabinetry, and finish work. The garage was also the owners' responsibility, as was the engaging of a contractor and crew to put the shell together.

Because the weather had turned extremely cold, there was a delay in pouring the foundation, but fortunately a January thaw gave the mason enough time to get the concrete poured before the return of freezing temperatures.

The bulk of the package arrived one cold February morning on the back of a flatbed truck and was promptly unloaded by the contractor's crew. Unfortunately, this turned out to be the last prompt service in the course of that contractor's work. After several months and several disputes, the contractor left the construction site and the owners were forced to find another builder.

Once that was accomplished, everything went more smoothly, although, as with any custom-built house, hundreds of decisions had to be made. "Elizabeth and I," says Lary, "spent countless weekends and evenings at lumberyards and places carrying plumbing and lighting fixtures, cabinetry, and so on."

It was decided to heat the house with forced warm air, but instead of breaking up the open plan with interior partitions to accommodate the heating ducts, it was decided to leave them exposed. Elizabeth was a bit apprehensive about doing this, but when the ducts—large columns well over 20 inches in diameter—were installed and painted a glossy slate blue, everyone agreed that they fitted perfectly into the post-and-beam atmosphere, lending a high-tech, sculptural quality to the house's soaring spaces.

A few months later than planned, and more than a few dollars over budget, Lary and Elizabeth moved into their new home. Some things, such as the third-floor loft and exterior painting, were to be finished later.

They felt that they had learned many things during the building experience—among them the difference between blueprints (even detailed engineering plans) and reality. As the kitchen began to take shape, for example, they realized that the layout was not as convenient and well organized as they wanted it to be—and also that there was not adequate space for their large refrigerator. The kitchen plan had to be revised and work that had already been done, redone. There had also been problems with installing the septic system, due to the slope of the terrain. The heavy additional cost proved a major blow to the budget.

Once moved in, Lary says, "there were surprises everywhere—most of them nice ones—including being able to see all the way up to the loft and cupola from the living/dining room." The openness of the space lends a warm informality to the house that pleases both Elizabeth and Lary and their guests. The quality of light is superb, giving the house a very upbeat feeling. And the view, as promised, is wonderful. From their satisfied perspective, the owners have come to two conclusions: one, they recommend a barn house; and two, they hope they never have to build another.

Close-up view of decorative, exposed heating ducts that run through second floor. Bedroom opens onto private balcony with same extensive view as from deck below. Skylights over bed on east side bring in morning sun. (Photo by Tom Hopkins.)

Built in the 1870s, this former dairy barn on one of the original homesteads in Clay County, Kansas, is now a comfortable home for the Mohlers and daughter Blair, now three years old. Old wagon entrance is now a glass-paneled front entry. The tiny windows on right side of barn were not only used for ventilating the hayloft, but are said by local historians to have served as gun ports in case of attack by Indians. They are now glassed in. (Photo by Thad Allton, Topeka Capital-Journal.)

DEB AND MARK MOHLER

"We live out here in the wilderness and love it."

———————◆———————

In 1983, when Mark and Deb Mohler purchased their ninety-five-acre farm in Clay County, Kansas, they had planned to build a log house. There was an old stone house on the property, but it was far too small for their needs. And the old limestone dairy barn, with its 18-inch-thick walls, was in very poor condition.

They changed their minds about the log house when they found the price of the unit they wanted had "shot up to $60,000"—way above what they could afford. That convinced Mark that renovating the old barn might be their best bet.

At first Deb was not too keen on the idea. The thought of living in a place where "barn owls were nesting" did not appeal to her. "They would not go away," she said. "They would leave little moles with heads off all over the place." Also, there was an 18-inch-thick accumulation of hardened manure on the lower level that had rotted out the floor planks, and the roof had been partially destroyed by a lightning-caused fire. So she was somewhat relieved when the estimate for the renovation came in at $80,000—far beyond their budgeted price.

But Mark was not discouraged. He knew that the barn could be made into a comfortable home, and he knew how he wanted to use the space, so he went ahead and drew up plans.

Then, by good fortune, he found just the right contractor—Mike Macender. "He was really interested in the project," Mark said. "The other contractors I talked with didn't really want to tackle the old barn—they were mostly interested in building new houses."

Macender was fascinated by the history of old barns and the Mohler barn was one of the original homesteads in Clay County. It was built around 1870 by Henry Elias, farmer, stonemason, and sawmill operator. For a time, the Elias family had lived in the third-floor hayloft of the barn, with their cows and pigs occupying the lower levels.

The Mohlers explained to Macender that they wanted to use the original materials wherever possible. "We wanted to preserve the old oak timbers that were joined with wood pegs or square nails, and especially the 36-foot-long hand-hewn main girder."

After the contractor had looked over the plans and inspected the barn, he said he could do the renovation for $30,000, if Mark and Deb would do some of the work. This seemed like a satisfactory arrangement, so in March of 1987 they began.

Mark, an area manager for the Kansas Fish and Game Commission, was used to hard outdoor work, but Deb, a teacher in Clay County schools, found some of it pretty hard going. During the course of the renovation she lost about fifteen pounds. They worked evenings and weekends and got help from friends whenever they could.

First, they had to clear out the barn and dig out the old manure from the lower-level floor with pick and shovel. In all, they hauled about sixty truckfuls of junk and debris out of the barn.

When Mark was ripping up the rotted floor planks on the lower level—the planks that had so recently been covered with manure—he discovered a cut-stone floor underneath. They decided to move the stones outside for a patio and to replace them with a poured concrete floor. "Some of the stones weighed 350 to 400 pounds," Mark recalls. "We'd pry them up with a bar, chip off the corners, and roll them outside."

In the old corral near the barn, they found some oak boards that they used for the interior woodwork in the living room. Old planks were also used for the kitchen ceiling, and the old siding from a springhouse on the farm was turned into paneling for the master bedroom. A section of heavy oak that once supported the ceiling over a doorway on the lower level was used for the fireplace mantel.

The large barn doors, where wagons once rolled in and out, were made into an attractive, light-filled, front entryway by surrounding the new wooden door with several wood-framed glass panels.

Because they didn't want to make any additional openings in the thick stone walls, they framed and glassed in all existing openings and installed skylights on the roof at the rear to provide more light. The narrow, slotlike openings in what is now the living room (which were traditionally cut into old stone barns for ventilation) were glassed in and now serve as tiny windows, large enough to peek out of, but convenient, too, as niches for small plants. Debbie says it's fun to come home at night and "see all twenty of these little windows lighted up." Local historians told them that these little slots also served as gun ports in case of attack by Indians.

The kitchen, appropriately enough, is where milking stalls once were. The cook can be part of the action in the living room, with its 19-foot double-height ceiling. Stairs lead to a guest room, formerly a hayloft. All timbers are oak from original framing. (Photo by Thad Allton, Topeka Capital-Journal.)

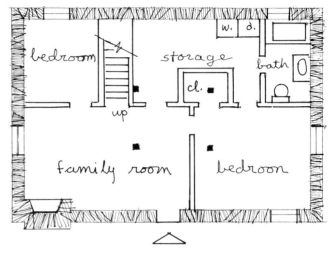

FIRST FLOOR: *Since cattle were once housed in this area, the ceilings were relatively low. The Mohlers decided to use this level for two bedrooms, a family room, a laundry/storage area, and a bath. A fireplace was added in the family room. (Illustration by Mary Lohmann.)*

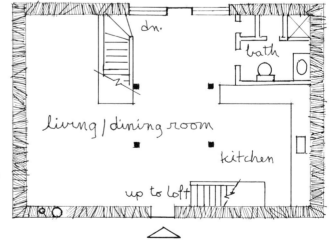

SECOND FLOOR: *Living room with 23½-foot-high ceiling was former hayloft. Kitchen and bathroom were former milking stalls. Kitchen is divided from living room by half partition so cook can be part of living room activity. (Illustration by Mary Lohmann.)*

There were three doors on the lower level. One of these doors is now an opening for a fireplace in the family room, one is still used as a door, and the third was made into a combination window and bookcase in the master bedroom.

The Mohlers wanted to leave the interior surface of the limestone walls exposed, but found that the stone flaked. The solution turned out to be a rubberlike substance originally designed for use on grain elevators. It was applied over the walls with an airless pump to seal the stone.

The lower level, where the cows once lived, was transformed into a spacious family room, two bedrooms, and a large bath/laundry/storage room. On the second level, with its 19-foot ceiling, are the living room, kitchen, and bath. A loft bedroom above the kitchen overlooks the living room—the same hayloft where the Elias family lived more than a hundred years ago.

The renovation that began in March was completed in July when Mark and Deb moved into their new barn house home. And because they had done so much of the work themselves—$15,000 worth of work—the total cost was only $32,000, a modest enough price for a comfortable and spacious home and for the preservation of a historic building.

The last time we spoke to Deb on the phone she told us about all the wonderful wildlife that comes around their barn house—deer, bobcats, rabbits, flocks of wild turkeys, quail, and pheasant. Their property is bounded on one side by thousands of acres of Fish and Game Wildlife Preserve and on the other side by property belonging to Fort Riley that "no one ever uses, so we live out here in the wilderness and love it."

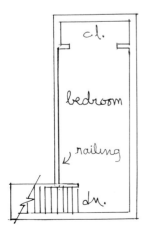

THIRD-FLOOR LOFT: *Bedroom loft is directly above kitchen and overlooks living room. This former hayloft was where the Elias family once lived when the barn was built in 1886. (Illustration by Mary Lohmann.)*

Main entry off porch opens to living/dining room. Wood-burning fireplace is on left as you enter. Stairs to master bedroom and railed balcony are next to fireplace. (Photo by Michael Shopenn.)

NANCY FRANKEN

"Three months . . . from the day they raised the frame . . . until I moved my furniture in."

———◦∞◦———

Nancy Franken says, "I've always wanted to live in a barn and would have loved to buy and renovate an old one, but the cost was prohibitive. So I decided to build a new barn house."

A native Washingtonian, Nancy knew the area well and found the property for her barn house on Bainbridge Island, a short ferryboat commute to Seattle, where she works. The site offered two acres of meadowland on what had once been part of a large dairy farm, people she knew, and a chance to be part of a van pool for the daily ferryboat ride to work—perfect for all her needs.

"I had a very clear picture of what I wanted," Nancy says, and none of the builders she talked with seemed just right to build the timber frame house she had in mind. Then, through a friend, she heard about Timbercraft Homes, Judith and Charles Landau's firm, which specializes in custom-built post-and-beam wood-joinery houses. Nancy went over to nearby Port Washington to meet and talk with the Landaus. "The minute I walked into their home," she says, "I knew they were the people I wanted to build my place."

She and Judith Landau worked together to design the house just as she saw it. It was not to be a large house, but comfortable and convenient. She wanted a barnlike openness with exposed timbers, reminiscent of an early western barn. And it was to have the kind of interior space that would nicely set off her collection of European folk art, including a handsome painted antique German armoire.

The 1,600 square feet of space was thoughtfully divided to include a large, two-story living room with a fireplace and a library alcove, a country kitchen, and a guest room and bath on the first floor. On the second floor, there was to be the master bedroom and bath with a balcony overlooking the living room. The plan also included a deck off the kitchen for outdoor living space and a western-style front porch to shelter the entryway. The house was to be oriented on the site so as to receive natural light all day as the sun moved from east to west.

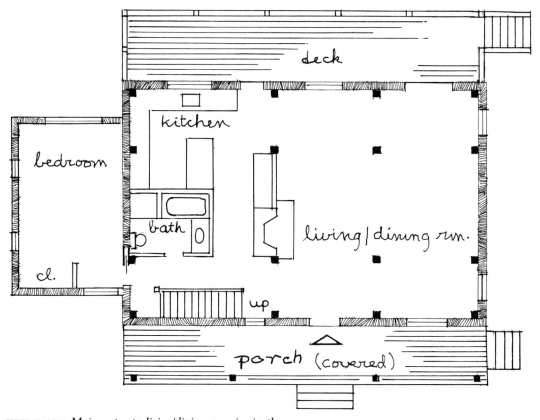

FIRST FLOOR: *Main entry to living/dining area is via the porch, protected by roof overhang. Bathroom with washer/dryer is located in easy reach of living area and kitchen as well as downstairs bedroom, which is an addition to the post-and-beam main house. (Illustration by Mary Lohmann.)*

The Timbercraft crew really pushed to complete the $120,000 barn house. Nancy had to leave the place she was renting and didn't want to make a temporary in-between move just for a few weeks or months. "They were fantastic," she says. "Three months, would you believe? From the day they raised the frame, until I moved my furniture in!"

The exterior of the barn house is board-and-batten cedar, left unstained to weather naturally—"Like an old barn," Nancy says. With its barn-red trim and steeply pitched roof, the building could indeed have been on the place for a long time. With its vaulted ceilings and 8-by-8 mortised-and-tenoned timbers joined with wooden pegs, the interior is a handsome example of the revival of the timber frame method of building.

Nancy Franken will have been in her barn house just four years in August 1991, but is so delighted with it that she feels as though she has lived there for a much longer time. The house is a marvelous showcase for Timbercraft Homes, too, and Nancy is happy to show it off and tell others about her pleasant experience working with the Landaus.

SECOND FLOOR: *This is very much the owner's domain, with stairs from the first floor leading directly to the master bedroom suite. Bedroom also opens onto study/loft and balcony overlooking living room. (Illustration by Mary Lohmann.)*

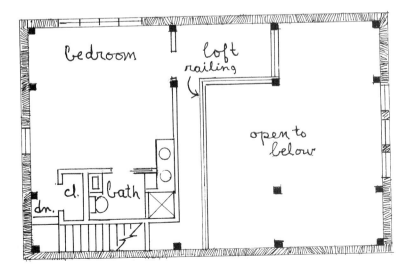

Barn house with south side is on slight rise, looks out beyond clearing over stand of evergreens. Broad span of windows brings in plenty of light to first floor. Skylights in roof light bedrooms on second floor for sons Matthew, fifteen, and Justin, twelve. Easy-to-install metal prefab chimney is for wood-burning stove in living room. (Photo by Eberhard Luethke.)

NANCY AND GARY MIERS

"It really bowled them over."

———— ❦ ————

Nancy and Gary Miers of Gray, Maine, had wanted a house for a long time, but like so many young couples today, knew that wanting a house and affording it were a long way apart. They had two children and were living in a rental unit in a town near where they had recently purchased five acres of woodland. They were ready to get going.

The Mierses had heard about The Shelter Institute in Bath, Maine, a home-building school that offered hands-on courses in do-it-yourself building. Since this was apparently the only way they were going to get the kind of house they wanted, they decided to investigate. They found that everything they needed to know would be covered at the institute and that the emphasis was on post-and-beam construction, which is what they wanted (see chapter 10 for a discussion of work you can do yourself). They began fifteen weekends of commuting to Bath—a round-trip of ninety miles.

Some four months later, having completed the various courses, they were ready to begin building. But first they needed a construction loan. Impressed by the institute with the importance of having all facts and figures on paper, Nancy, a registered nurse, and Gary, a mechanical engineer, set about assembling in an orderly manner all the facts they would need to present their case to the bank. "I had everything," Gary says, "detailed plans, specifications, materials lists with costs, estimates for all work we couldn't handle ourselves—and then, the clincher, the completion-of-course certificate from The Shelter Institute. It really bowled them over."

The bank was so impressed with their presentation that it gave them a very favorable construction loan, one that would automatically become a mortgage without additional charges—points—as soon as they moved into the house.

They decided to buy the post-and-beam house kit designed and produced by The Shelter Institute because they liked the barnlike openness it provided and the look of the exposed timbers. And the price was right— $8,525. This included erection of the frame.

Maine winters are cold, but efficient stove keeps whole house warm, burning only five cords of wood a season. Stairs behind stove, leading to second floor, look in this photograph like a decorative architectural detail, but now have banisters, as does balcony above. Natural honey-colored pine supporting beams in ceiling add character to whole house. (Photo by Eberhard Luethke.)

Nancy and Gary made some adjustments in the basic plan to suit their needs. They also decided to add a stick-built saltbox addition along one wall to provide an entry hall and mud room, and to add more space to the kitchen and bathroom.

The only serious trouble they had during the entire course of construction was at the very beginning. Just after the trenches for the foundations had been dug, it rained for four days and the soil that had just

Looking from living room toward dining area and kitchen. Door straight ahead leads to master bedroom and bath. Door on left leads down to full basement, used now for storage and for possible future backup heating system. Once basement and foundations were in, the entire frame was erected by a crew of three in a day and a half. (Photo by Eberhard Luethke.)

been so laboriously dug out was washed right back into the trench. The whole thing had to be redug. After that, a dry spell assured smooth going, and the foundations were poured in September 1988.

Shortly afterward, a three-man crew from The Shelter Institute arrived with the components for the frame—8-by-8-inch and 8-by-10-inch posts and beams. Mortise-and-tenon joints had been precut, so it was now just a matter of lifting the timbers into position, fitting them together, and

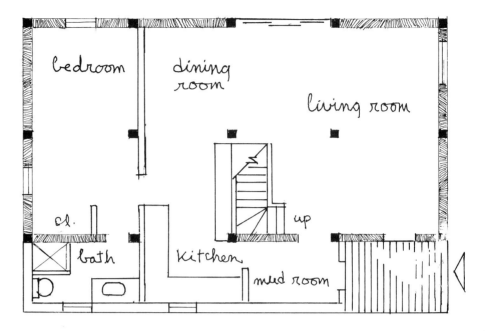

FIRST FLOOR: *The addition of a 6-by-31-foot shed-roof extension along the north wall made space for a mudroom, master bedroom, bath, and larger kitchen/dining area. It also changed the "boxy" look of the exterior to the more pleasing Saltbox line. Living room has 10-by-8-foot cathedral ceiling open to above. (Illustration by Mary Lohmann.)*

driving in the wood pegs to secure the joints. Steel hangers were included to fix the floor joists to the beams.

The frame was up in a day and a half. Then the Mierses took over. The first thing they wanted to do was to get the place weathered in for the winter, so they took three weeks off from their regular jobs to work full-time on the house. Once the roof, siding, windows, and doors were installed and their "vacation" was over, they worked evenings and weekends throughout the winter. They added 2-by-4 studding between the vertical posts and applied fiberglass insulation between the studs. By using this method of insulation they lost about four inches from the exposed posts on the interior walls, but it produced an energy-efficient house.

They then installed the interior partitions and had a plumber rough in the water supply and drain lines. The wiring was done by Gary, who had learned the technique at The Shelter Institute. And they installed the

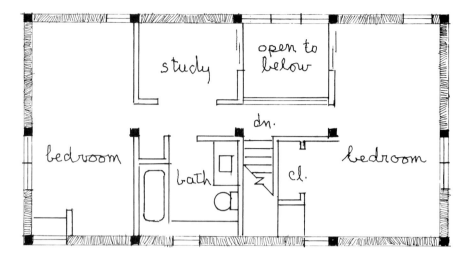

SECOND FLOOR: *Centrally located hall provides good access to bath from the two bedrooms and study. Southwest end of hall overlooks living room. (Illustration by Mary Lohmann.)*

drywall—a job that requires much nailing, taping, application of joint compound, sanding, and patience.

In April 1989, they moved in. They still had a lot of finish work to do, but they could at last stop paying rent and interest on their construction loan. This would now be converted to a mortgage.

When we visited the house that July, we were impressed with the airy, light-filled atmosphere and, though it is not a large house, the feeling of spaciousness the open ceilings give. We were really impressed by the Mierses. Their dedication had produced an attractive three-bedroom, two-bath home for a modest amount of money at a time when most other couples were bemoaning the fact that they couldn't find an affordable home.

When we talked in the spring of 1990, Gary allowed that they were almost, but not quite, finished. One of the major items they plan to add is an oil-fired baseboard hot-water heating system. At present they use a wood stove for heat and it has kept the place comfortable, but, as Gary says, "The trouble with a wood stove is that you can't get away for very long unless you want to take the chance of the pipes freezing because the stove ran out of wood."

Nancy and Gary feel a real sense of accomplishment when they look at their house. "It's a great feeling," Nancy said, "and we're not ashamed to say we walk around and admire our work with a lot of pride and satisfaction." Part of the satisfaction probably comes from getting that much house—2,000 square feet—for a total cost of $54,586.49.

ITEMIZED COST FIGURES

1.	Post-and-beam frame kit and labor to erect	$ 8,525.00
2.	Excavation (including removing tree stumps, foundation hole, well trench, foundation drainage system, septic system installation, driveway, and final grading)	10,866.66
3.	Foundation and basement floor	5,246.50
4.	Well installation	3,122.40
5.	All other building materials (including framing, sheathing, siding, roofing, drywall, paint, electrical supplies)	17,990.78
6.	Windows and skylight	3,738.26
7.	Water pump and installation	1,415.00
8.	Plumber	2,386.31
9.	Linoleum installation	1,079.00
10.	Ceramic tiles (kitchen counters)	216.58
		$54,586.49

THE PEABODY BARN HOUSE

"It was sort of slanting."

———❧———

Converting an old barn into a comfortable home was a natural for Betsy and Bill Peabody. Bill had lived on a farm for many years, had previously owned one, and "liked the feeling of a barn atmosphere." Betsy, an enthusiastic horsewoman, loved open spaces, a feeling of being able to expand, and the idea of combining something old with the new and contemporary. They both sparked to the idea of rescuing one of a disappearing breed—the beautiful antique barns of New England—so many of which were just "falling to the ground." It was also a way of preserving a bit of history. So, the Peabodys, both of whom are family therapists in Woodstock, Vermont, began to look around the area for a suitable barn to move to a rolling spread of hilltop acreage they had recently purchased outside of town.

The barn that seemed just right was finally spotted about fifteen miles away. "It was sort of slanting," says Betsy, but still looked worth investigating. They had heard of The Barn People, local craftspeople experienced in the restoration of antique wood-frame structures, and contacted them to do a feasibility study of the barn. After a thorough inspection of the frame, David Hill and Ken Epworth, two of the partners in the firm, agreed that since most of the heavy timbers were sound, the 30-by-38-foot hay barn was indeed worthy of the time, expense, and painstaking work it would take to dismantle the old frame, clean and repair the timbers, and truck them to the new site. Once there, they would be re-erected as the antique core of the Peabodys' new barn house. The Barn People were to take it down, get the timbers in good shape, add any new timber necessary, and re-erect the frame. Before this could be done, however, a basement had to be excavated and a masonry foundation built.

In the meantime, the Peabodys were working out the final plans with the builder/contractor who would take over after the frame was up. They consulted an architect, who approved their ideas and drew up the floor plans and the elevations, but they did most of the planning themselves. For the past several years, they had been scanning magazines and making sketches of the special things they wanted incorporated in their barn house.

On entering kitchen and living/dining area, eyes go immediately to the Finnish stove on its soapstone-topped raised hearth. The stove radiates heat to the entire core space. An open fireplace with matching raised hearth is in living room wall behind stove. A small baking oven with firebox unit and wood-storage niche beneath is also in this wall. All doors in this part of the barn house have curved tops, repeating the curve of the Finnish stove. (Photos by Tom Hopkins.)

They had also been studying possible traffic patterns and room arrangements, so they knew just what they wanted.

High on the want list was a "Finnish stove." Bill had seen a feature story in *American Home* magazine some years before and had been so impressed with the attractiveness, efficiency, and energy-saving features of this stove that he was determined to have one in their new home. The builder of the stove happened to live in southwestern Vermont but declined to come to Woodstock, saying it was too far. Instead, he gave Bill the name of a mason/stove expert nearby who agreed to build it. The Finnish stove, a focal point in the living room of the finished barn house, is a remarkable-looking domed concrete monolith. Painted white, it is one of the first things to catch the eye upon entering the open-ceilinged living room/dining area. Except for the shed-roof additions, the stove heats the entire house.

On the second floor is a large studio, a bath, and a large bedroom. These are connected by a railed balcony open to the dining room below. Plenty of space is also allotted for storage on this level. The stairwells on this floor and on the first floor leading to the basement/lounge are lined with finely milled maple bookshelves.

Downstairs, on the basement level, is another concrete monolith containing the firebox for the stove system, which is stoked with wood. There is also an exercise room, sauna, bath, and large storage area on this level. As backup heat to the Finnish stove, the Peabodys have a baseboard circulating-hot-water system, which heats the shed additions and the heating coils under the living room floor. This is turned on by an automatic thermostat if the stove is allowed to go out, or if the family is away in the winter.

The project got off to a slow start because excavating for the basement and foundation proved more difficult than anticipated. Ledge rock was found, so a good deal of blasting had to be done before the masonry work could begin. Once begun, however, the rest of the work began to hum along nicely. With the revitalized timber frame now in place, the contractor and crew could begin building the shed-roof additions, which would be stud-built. Included in these first-floor additions would be a 12-by-42-foot master bedroom suite with a large bath and walk-in closet, and a 12-by-21-foot studio on the north side, where Bill would have good light for his painting. There would also be a good-sized laundry, a half bath, a pantry, and a 12-by-18-foot screened porch to be entered from a wood deck on

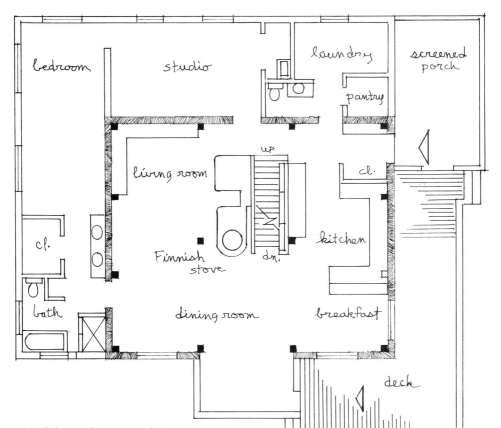

FIRST FLOOR: *Shaded area shows original 30-by-38-foot antique barn frame where kitchen, dining room, and living room are now located. The entire area is heated by the Finnish stove, which is strategically positioned to serve all three rooms. Master bedroom and bath, studio, laundry, and half bath are part of stud-built addition, heated by baseboard circulating hot water, which is also standby heat for the rest of the house. Main entry is from screened porch that opens onto deck. (Illustration by Mary Lohmann.)*

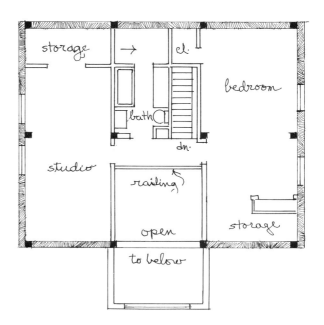

SECOND FLOOR: *Second bedroom, studio, and bath are also within original old frame. Connecting balcony between bedroom and studio is open to below and overlooks dining room. (Illustration by Mary Lohmann.)*

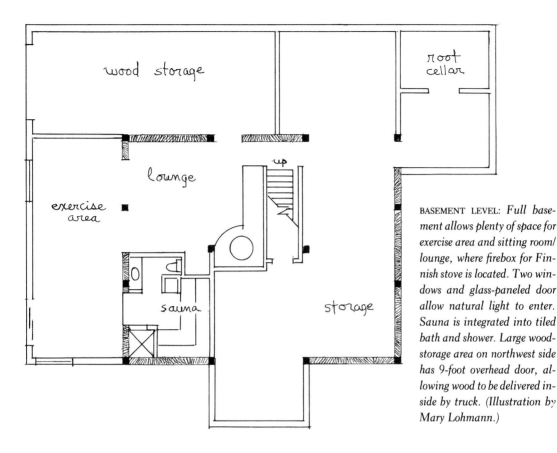

BASEMENT LEVEL: *Full basement allows plenty of space for exercise area and sitting room/lounge, where firebox for Finnish stove is located. Two windows and glass-paneled door allow natural light to enter. Sauna is integrated into tiled bath and shower. Large wood-storage area on northwest side has 9-foot overhead door, allowing wood to be delivered inside by truck. (Illustration by Mary Lohmann.)*

the east side of the house. Leading from the screened porch would be the main entry door.

Bill, a good amateur carpenter, worked on the house all the way through, along with the carpenters. He had arranged his business affairs so that he could be on the site and available to make immediate decisions when required. He and Betsy figured that this not only insured that things would be done right the first time, but saved time, money, and headaches.

The finished barn house is absolutely stunning. A love for fine woods and fine woodworking is evident everywhere—from the dark honey tone of the antique pegged timbers to the lighter glow of the maple trim framing the tall casement windows. The kitchen cabinets are also of maple, as is the handsome floor in the living room. Attention to detail has obviously been of great importance to the Peabodys. And it shows in both small and large ways. All doorframes in the living/dining area, for example, are rounded at the top, repeating the curve of the domed Finnish stove.

Adjacent to the Finnish stove, which is on a raised blue-gray soapstone-topped hearth, is a fireplace wall with space not only for a rounded-top fireplace, on a similar raised hearth, but for a small baking oven with its own firebox underneath. Under this is a storage space for wood. The oven is convenient to the kitchen, so that Betsy, an accomplished baker, can keep an eye on her home-baked goodies.

Mexican tile is used for flooring in the dining room and kitchen and is in cheerfully warm contrast to the lighter wood used to frame the double-height windows in the dining room. With its southern exposure and the generous use of glass, this entire first floor is flooded with light. Needless to say, views of the lovely Vermont hills from all these windows are spectacular. And standing on the broad deck outside, breathing in the clean mountain air is a delight. So is this splendid barn house that Bill and Betsy built.

Asked if he had any words of warning or wisdom for would-be barn house builders, Bill Peabody had this to say: "Embarking on any house building, better make sure your relationship and marriage is pretty good." Also, he added, "Have plenty of money."

THE JOHNSON BARN

". . . happily raised three daughters and numerous four-legged creatures."

The old barn that Vicki and Garnie Johnson have converted into an attractive and comfortable home at Triple J Farms in Sterling, Colorado, has had an interesting past, to say the least.

The balloon frame, gambrel-roof barn was built in 1926 as a horse-and-hay barn for Vicki's great-uncle, Conrad Yost, and his wife, Ella.

When the barn was half completed and not yet properly braced, it was struck by a small tornado and extensively damaged (see photos). It took many days of hard work to get the barn set straight again so it could be finished. Friends and neighbors came over to give a hand and help shingle the roof.

Half-finished balloon frame barn after being hit by tornado in 1926. (Photo by the Johnson family.)

Friends and neighbors give a hand shingling the large expanse of roof after barn was set straight and framing was completed. (Photo by the Johnson family.)

Barn shortly after it had been moved onto new foundation. The horizontal line running through the middle row of windows shows where the top was cut off so the barn could fit under a highway overpass. (Photo by the Johnson family.)

The Johnsons' barn house today. The major change to the exterior was the addition of two dormers. Otherwise, if it were not for the bright red-painted siding and white trim, Conrad Yost would recognize it as the barn he built over sixty-five years ago. The barn is much more roomy than it appears, since all three floors are in use. Deck added increases living space. Considerable landscaping has been done since this picture was taken. (Photo by the Johnson family.)

Vicki had always loved the barn, so in 1974, when her great-aunt gave it to her, she and Garnie decided to move it to their horse farm, where they raised "sport horses" (used as jumpers) and show-quality miniature horses. They would then renovate it into a home for themselves and their three daughters.

Garnie took on the chore of preparing the barn for the thirty-five-mile journey to Sterling, near the South Platte River. The upper half of the barn had to be cut off so the load would fit under the overpass on the interstate highway that led to Sterling. It would be put back on after the lower half was set on a foundation at the new site. Garnie also had to

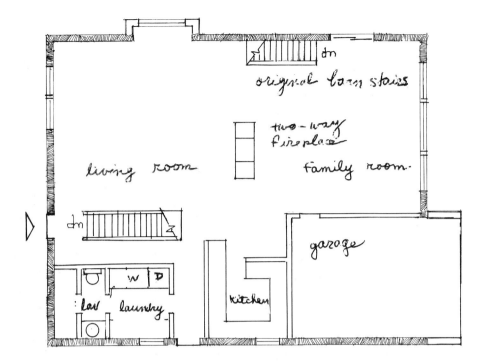

FIRST FLOOR: *Two-way fireplace serves both living and family rooms. Dining area is close to kitchen. Stairs in family room lead to second-floor lounge and were original stairs in old barn. Entry leads to main stairway up. Garage opens into family room, convenient for carrying supplies to kitchen. (Illustration by Mary Lohmann.)*

brace the structure to make certain it would not again suffer the damage it had when the tornado hit it. After the preparation work was completed, the house movers took over, and for $1,100 got the two halves of the barn safely to its new site.

The Johnsons turned the renovation work over to a general contractor, Byron Franz of nearby Windsor. Franz had built a barn house on his own, so they felt he was well qualified to handle their job. Franz proved to be "an imaginative and innovative contractor," according to Vicki. "He really got to know our family, so it was all very personalized."

Renovations began in July and were completed the following March, at a total cost of $80,000.

The outside configuration of the original barn was kept intact. Inside, the 2,500 square feet of space was divided into three floors. The first floor

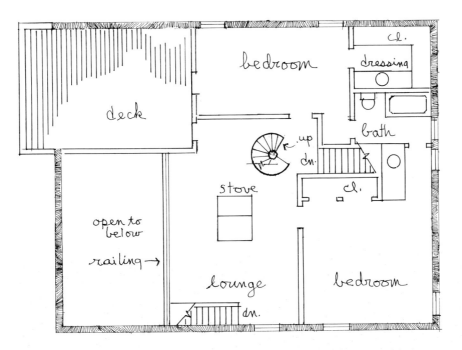

SECOND FLOOR: *Deck built over garage is reached from lounge and from second bedroom. Lounge, with centrally located wood stove, overlooks family room. Spiral stairs lead to third floor. (Illustration by Mary Lohmann.)*

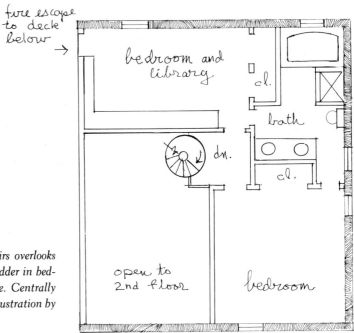

THIRD FLOOR: *Landing at top of stairs overlooks lounge on second floor. Fire escape ladder in bedroom/library leads to deck over garage. Centrally located bath serves both bedrooms. (Illustration by Mary Lohmann.)*

Front door enters directly into living room and open stairway, which leads to lounge on second floor. Plant-filled antique sleigh is showcased against picture window. (Photo by the Johnson family.)

(ground level) includes a living room, a family room, a two-way fireplace, and a kitchen, laundry, and lavatory. The garage opens into the family room.

The second floor has two bedrooms, one of them opening onto a deck over the garage; a bathroom; and a lounge that overlooks the family room below.

The third floor is reached via a spiral staircase from the second floor, and contains two more bedrooms and a bath. The space is open to the lounge below.

The house is furnished with the many antiques the Johnsons have collected over the years, including an antique horse-drawn sleigh that now has its home in the living room and is filled with seasonal flowers, greens, and gifts at holiday times.

Shortly after they moved into their renovated barn, the Johnsons received a letter signed by fourteen members of the Yost family, giving a brief history of the old barn. The letter ended: "The previous owners of the old barn wish for the Johnsons many, many happy years in their new home. May God's blessings rest on them always."

Their blessings have been many, as Vicki wrote us in 1990, fifteen years later. "We have happily raised three daughters and numerous four-legged creatures. . . . Our girls have raised and shown horses here along the South Platte River. And now that the youngest is going off to college, I am in the process of making the barn into a "Bales and Breakfast" establishment—offering bed, breakfast, and stabling facilities for traveling horse people."

"Before" picture of Jill Butler's barn before it was dismantled. (Photo by Craig Rowley.)

JILL BUTLER

"I know . . . this is a Jill space."

———◇———

Jill Butler, artist and textile and home furnishings designer, who heads her own design firm in New York, had been renting a weekend place in a small town in Connecticut where she could unwind and work on the paintings and collages that were her private pleasure. A barn lover ever since she was a little girl growing up in the farm country outside of Kalamazoo, Michigan, Jill had recently found what she thought would be a perfect site on which to build a barn house—a 7½-acre parcel of land near the Connecticut River. The fact that the land had a house on it didn't faze her—she immediately sold it off to get "barn money" and start things rolling.

Shortly thereafter, she went over to the local art gallery to talk with the owners about an exhibit of her work that was soon to open. They were chatting with an old friend, Craig Rowley, a restorationist/builder who was fresh from a meeting with a client who wanted a house restored. Introduced with, "Here's a lady who is looking for an old barn to convert," Jill and Rowley hit if off immediately. He had just heard of an antique barn for sale in a town some thirty-five miles away and, after seeing some of Rowley's work in the portfolio he had just shown his client, Jill agreed to go with him the next day, to look at the barn.

What they found was a handsome 36-by-27-foot barn, built around 1800. The roof and siding were not in great shape, but the chestnut timbers of the frame were in excellent condition. The barn seemed perfect for Jill's purpose, so on Rowley's advice, she decided to buy it.

The following day, it was hers—for $3,000. Rowley was to dismantle the structure and truck the timbers to the site she had chosen on her newly acquired land. He and his crew would erect the frame and then, acting as general contractor, he would complete the barn house.

During the dismantling process, after the old roofing and siding were removed and discarded, photographs of the frame were taken and each timber was measured. This data would be used to build a scale model, which would help in the reassembly and with the planning of the interior. Some two weeks later, Rowley and his crew had completed the dismantling and had labeled, color-coded, and cleaned each timber, hauled away the debris, and trucked everything to the new site. This added $10,000 to the original barn price. Now would begin the process of putting it all back together again, but first, preparations had to be made for the 1,000-square-foot basement that Jill needed for a workshop and storage area. Considerable excavation work had to be done, so it was not until the end of the summer that the concrete footings and foundation basement walls could be poured. After that, it took Rowley and his crew only two weeks to erect the frame.

A few days later, Rowley called Jill to tell her that the frame was up, although not yet thoroughly braced, and also that a hurricane was expected to hit the area the next day. A good test of the barn's stability, Jill thought. And indeed it was. High winds had uprooted "a lot of trees ranging over the rafters," says Jill, "but the structure came through fine."

Now that the frame was erected, Jill and Rowley could better visualize exactly how to plan the space. Jill went all over Connecticut photographing old barns so as to have a better feel of the many details that make a barn a barn. Maintaining the integrity of the basic structure was important to both of them. She had a scrapbook of ideas from magazines and a workbook with loads of original ideas of her own. The guiding motif was, keep it barnlike, keep it simple—lots of open space, lots of lighting; a place for work and a place for play.

After several months, and many telephone calls to New York when Jill couldn't make it to Connecticut, the interior layout began to take shape. The 36-foot length of the original barn proved inadequate to provide enough space for Jill's studio and the spacious living, dining, and kitchen areas she also wanted, so a 13-by-27-foot shed-roof extension was built on the west end of the frame. This would include a skylight for the studio as well as an entryway and stairs to the basement.

The roof, at its apex, was raised almost the length of the barn so that a line of clerestory windows could be installed to admit more natural light to the upper levels. Simple barn-style windows were used where needed, and in order to keep windows at a minimum and maintain the plain barn look, skylights were used as much as possible. For the same reason, no attempt was made to conceal the electric wiring, which was encased in rigid metal conduits, painted white, and run up the walls to the various levels. "It looks very simple," Jill says, "which is the way it's supposed to

Clerestory windows and skylight in roof bring light to main bedroom. Note built-in storage drawers under bed, closets on either side of bed. (Photo by Tom Hopkins.)

look. Most people bury all the wires but this is the traditional barn solution. It's also high-tech."

Jill wanted to use plain pine boards for the interior walls and leave the structural timbers exposed to their full depth. Rowley's solution was to first install the pine boards on the outside of the frame. Over these, on the exterior, he applied 2-inch high-density insulation board, then ½-inch plywood sheathing, a wind barrier over that, and, finally, tongue-and-groove vertical siding.

On the south side of the barn house, a pair of tall glass-paned French

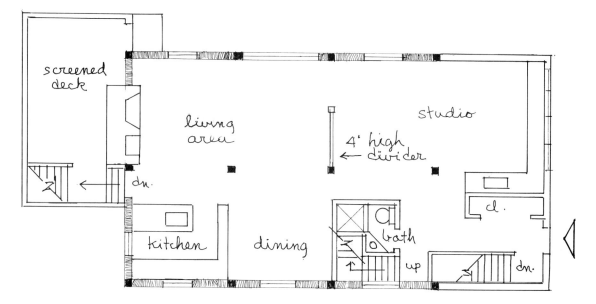

FIRST FLOOR: *A 13-foot shed-roof extension was added to provide space for side entry, stairs, and a larger studio. Skylights set in roof allow natural light into studio. A 4-foot divider is set between studio and living room, but since it is not much more than counter-height, it doesn't affect sense of openness. Dining alcove and alley to glass door in center are open to levels above. Original barn frame is indicated by shaded lines. Small black squares indicate original posts. (Illustration by Mary Lohmann.)*

doors, flanked on either side by more glass panels, were installed in what had been the former hay wagon entrance. This treatment, which is a focal point in the downstairs area, floods the entire living room/studio/dining alcove with light and adds to the dramatic effect of double-height ceilings. The French doors lead outside to a wooden deck and stone terrace.

On the east side of the living room, a wood-framed fireplace was added. The kitchen, which is open to the living room and dining alcove, is partially screened on the living room side by a half partition with open shelves for dishes and glasses. A slightly lower counter acts as a pass-through to the dining alcove.

Above the studio/living areas are five interconnected loft spaces, some just a few steps above or below the others. The effect is totally unexpected, and as Rowley describes the way he and Jill worked it out, "We sort of molded the space to fit the frame." The description seems very apt as you go upstairs to a small sitting room/guest room with television and audio equipment, nestled into the roof rafters over the studio area. If you want

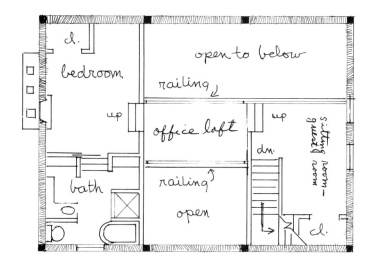

SECOND FLOOR: *Plan indicates four different levels—sitting/guest room, office/loft, master bedroom, and bath. Loft and sitting room overlook living room. All levels are reached from stairs in small hall next to entry door. A fifth level, a small sleeping loft (not shown on plan), was added as an afterthought near the roof peak. (Illustration by Mary Lohmann.)*

to see what's going on downstairs, there are a couple of small panels you can slide open and poke your head through.

Up a few more steps is Jill's office, complete with telephone, typewriter, and fax machine, which Jill uses to communicate with the outside world—including Paris, where she has many interests and to which she commutes regularly. Keep going and a few more steps lead to a tiny guest room just under the roof, with space for a bed and not much else.

You have now gone as far as you can, so it is time to cross the office level and go down a few steps to the master bedroom, where a pair of small skylights mounted over the bed bring in light and ventilation. Down a couple of steps is a large dressing room open to the bedroom. Beyond is a roomy enclosed bathroom. Imaginative use of a narrow skylight and a small, diamond-shaped window brings in natural light to both areas.

Back downstairs is the light-filled living/studio area, where pine-boarded walls washed with a thin coating of white paint offer a cool, airy-looking contrast to the warm golden brown of the old chestnut timbers, as do the wide pine-board floors, painted a glossy white. Jill's painting and collages add gaiety and color everywhere, and in the studio section, on an enormous white work table are neatly arranged tubes of paint, brushes, and other artist's supplies, testifying that this is indeed a work space.

Considering Jill's busy work schedule, and the fact that she was not always available to make important decisions when they came up, the year and a half it took to finish the barn house was really quite remarkable. Her admiration for Rowley and his handling of the entire job is immense. "Fortunately, Craig and I have similar taste, " Jill says, "so we could make a lot of decisions over the phone. And if I was not available, he would simply move to do some other work until we could get together."

Total cost of this 2,000-square-foot entirely custom project, from buying the old barn through completed barn house, was $385,000. This included some complicated and costly sitework, since there was considerable solid rock around the site that made installation of pipes and the septic system very difficult.

The last time we talked with Jill she had just renovated a sixteenth-century building in Normandy—which, she says, "feels very much like this," indicating the barn house where we were talking. "Everyone says, 'I know this is your space—this is a Jill space.' "

CHRIS AND TOM HOPKINS

" . . . post-and-beam concept, but was more simple."

———— ✺ ————

Chris and Tom Hopkins had an ideal site picked out for their new house: high ground overlooking a pond on twelve acres of wooded land Tom had bought in 1986.

Tom is a professional photographer, so their plan was to combine a large photographic studio with the house. But when the estimates came back, they found the plan was "a little too costly," Tom said. So they decided instead to build "an apartment-type home" on another site nearby, and resolved that "someday we would build another home on the pond." When they did, they could rent the smaller house.

Tom felt that a barn-style post-and-beam house would be the easiest to build, and that a kit would be easier to assemble than starting from scratch. After some searching they found a kit that seemed to fit their needs, a 30-by-36-foot barn/garage with a gambrel roof.

When the plans arrived, Tom and Chris, an artist and graphic designer for a utility company, reworked them to fit their need for more living space. They would have space for a workshop and garage by building a grade-level floor, and the original barn/garage plan would become the second-level living area. By raising the knee wall up three feet and by changing from a gambrel to a pitched roof, the living/dining and kitchen areas would now have a double-height open ceiling—high enough for a small loft level above the bedroom and bath to be included on the second level. A large deck off the living room would add even more space.

Tom assembled a crew of three, including his brother, an experienced carpenter/contractor. The others had all had some building experience.

When the kit was delivered they found that the timbers had not been cut to exact length. "They were all a foot or so longer than required," Tom says, "so we had to trim each one to size." At first they used a circular saw with a 10-inch-diameter blade, but soon discovered that a chain saw was faster and just as accurate.

The plans, according to Tom, "were not very good," and had no clear instructions as to how the timbers were to be assembled, so the crew worked out their own method—half-lap joints secured with 6-inch-long

spikes. "It was a sort of bastardized form of post-and-beam concept, but was more simple. None of us had ever done post and beam before so we just stumbled along at first. But once we got the knack of it, it turned out to be easier than conventional building."

The most difficult part of the job was installing the heavy 22-foot-long roof rafters. Tom finally hired a crane and operator to lift the rafters into position. "It cost $300 for the single day we needed the crane, but it was worth it," Tom said.

The plan provided no data on how to insulate the walls so that the beams could be left exposed on the inside. Once again, Tom and his crew had to work out their own method. They installed 2-by-6 stud walls on the outside of the frame, insulating between the studs and using drywall on the interior.

Although Tom modestly claims he was only "an expert helper," he worked right along with the others and handled much of the plumbing and wiring himself. One of the crew had been a plumber's assistant, and gave him advice and a hand with some of the plumbing. An electrician friend checked Tom's wiring every two weeks and did the final connections to the "box" (the circuit breaker panel) and also installed the electric service entrance system. "What I would do," Tom explained, "was to go ahead and do whatever had to be done, but always have an expert come over to check my work."

A surprising three months after the foundations were in, the barn house was completed and Tom and Chris could move in. It is a bright, airy, invitingly spacious home. The original barn/garage plan had only

Living room is on left as you enter. Steep pitch of roof is emphasized by the darker structural timbers silhouetted against the light pine ceiling. Boards for ceiling were given a wash of thinned-down white paint before they were put up. The paint solution (fifty parts paint to fifty parts paint thinner) was brushed on, left to seep in for five minutes, then wiped off with clean rags. Baskets hanging from beam were collected by Chris and Tom on trips to Africa, South America, and the Caribbean. Hutch next to bookcase is Irish country pine. Ladder leads to loft guest room. (Photo by Tom Hopkins.)

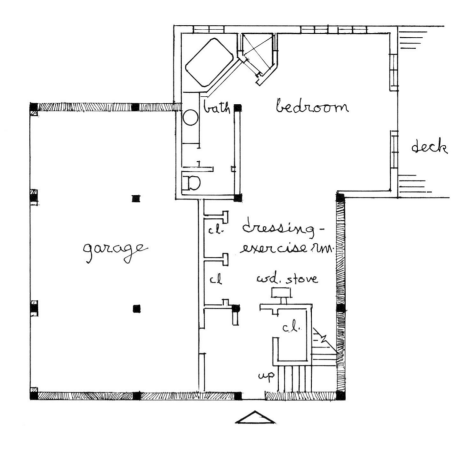

FIRST FLOOR: *As first floor was not included in original plan for barn/garage kit, it was built to accommodate a master bedroom/bath/dressing room/exercise area, plus the main entry to the second floor and a three-car garage. (Illustration by Mary Lohmann.)*

1,152 square feet, but by using that plan for the second level, instead of the grade level, and by raising the roof, this was increased to 1,400 square feet.

The plans shown here are newly reworked and are now in the process of being carried out due to an addition to the Hopkins family, Avery Elizabeth Hopkins, who arrived in late October 1990. The second-level space Chris and Tom are currently using as their bedroom is to be the nursery. A master bedroom and bath, a dressing room, and an exercise

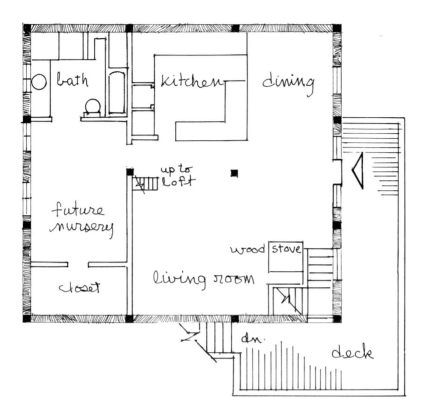

SECOND LEVEL: *By raising knee walls in original gambrel roof plan and changing to a pitched roof, enough space was created for a large living/dining/kitchen area, as well as for a bedroom (future nursery) and bath. The double-height ceiling allowed space for a small loft, used as an occasional guest bedroom. Outside entry is from deck. (Illustration by Mary Lohmann.)*

area are to be on the ground level. An entryway is planned for that level, but the main entrance will be upstairs, off the deck, as it is now.

The finished house cost $80,000. This included a well, the septic system, bringing in a road a half-mile long, and lines for electricity and telephone. The original project was financed with a construction loan, later converted to a $100,000 mortgage, which also covered an unpaid balance on the land. The new construction now in progress is expected to come to around $20,000.

This c. 1850 post-and-beam former dairy barn was completely renovated in 1985, and when viewed from the road side looks very much as it did when in use as a working barn. The wide entrance at front is actually seldom used; owners and guests prefer the convenience of the east entryway on the first level behind the barn. To preserve the traditional barn look of no (or few) windows on the north side, the architect instead brought light to that side of the house with the tall, glass-paneled door and rectangular fixed glass above. (Photo by Tom Hopkins.)

THE HOGANS

" . . . just as long as it's not an ordinary house."

When Pat and Tom Hogan bought their barn house in 1986 in a thriving New England river town, the barn had only recently been renovated. The Hogans, therefore, were the very first occupants—human, that is—to live in it.

The barn had been carefully and sensitively converted into a three-level dwelling with both soaring and cozy spaces and a convenient flow of traffic. The exposed chestnut posts and beams, roof rafters, and warm paneling of well-aged wood made for a home that anyone would hate to leave. Alas, the Hogans are going to have to sell the barn house and move to another state, where Tom's firm has recently transferred him.

But their barn house has spoiled them for living in a conventional house. "We're going to look for another barn to renovate or a firehouse, an old church, or whatever—just as long as it's not an ordinary house," Pat allowed.

The handsome three-bay post-and-beam barn had been built around 1850 as part of a large estate, and had for years housed dairy cows, a bull, and horses. There was also a loft to store the hay taken from nearby meadows. Now, almost 150 years later, the surrounding farmland has been replaced by many houses and the old barn is within easy walking distance of the village.

When the estate was broken up in 1984, the barn and one acre were purchased by then-resident Richard Bennett, who had admired the barn for years and thought it would make an attractive home. He decided to renovate the barn and then sell it. Bennett arranged with Chad Floyd, A.I.A., of Centerbrook Architects in Centerbrook, Connecticut, to design and plan the renovation. Architect James Coan of the same firm would serve as project manager.

Floyd did not wish to make any changes in the barnlike appearance of the structure, especially as viewed from the road. So the plans called for the front entry, for example, to be exactly where the original old barn doors had been. The old metal cupola that had provided ventilation to the barn was left in place on the roof and a power-driven fan was added.

Looking down from open (and balustraded) French doors of third-floor master bedroom to living room. The fireplace added on this east wall was faced with old chestnut planks, as was the second fireplace, added on the west wall of the dining room. Peering through these antique, wood-pegged timbers, it is not hard to imagine being back in the old hayloft. The many windows added on the south and east sides bring light in at various levels, as does the many-paned glass entrance on the north side. The double-height room benefits from light sources at these different levels. (Photo by Tom Hopkins.)

Chimneys were built for the two fireplaces and the central heating system but were encased in wood and painted the same light weathered gray as the siding, so as to be as unobtrusive as possible.

The interior space was also carefully designed to make the most efficient use of space while, at the same time, preserving the barnlike openness and giving maximum exposure to the beautiful century-and-a-

Staircase from living room leads to an intimate little sitting room on the third-floor level and then on to the master bedroom and bath. The white-painted stairs and balusters offer a fresh contrast to the exposed timbers and nicely point up the beauty of the old wood. Pat Hogan's folk art figures were arranged on stairs just for fun while the photographs were being taken. (Photo by Tom Hopkins.)

half-old chestnut and oak timbers so skillfully fitted together with wood joinery.

Plans also called for a view of the roof rafters from the two-story living room. A balcony sitting room on the third level overlooks the living area and provides a marvelous opportunity for a close-up inspection of all the timbers and joints, from purlins to struts to roof boards.

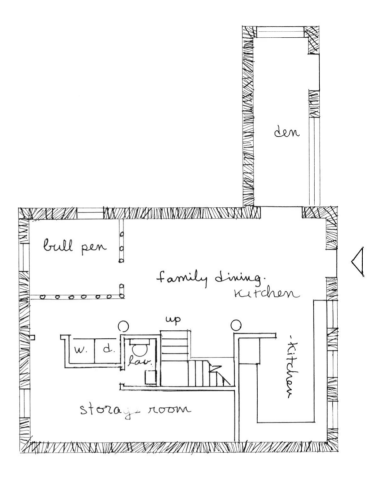

FIRST FLOOR: *Side entry, convenient to driveway and parking, leads into family/dining/kitchen area and to stairs up to second floor. Old bull pen still has iron bars but is more than a conversation piece—Pat Hogan uses it to display the large examples of her American folk art. The den, now a comfortable retreat, was a former manure shed. It's also used as a guest room. (Illustration by Mary Lohmann.)*

After the plans had been approved by the owner, a contractor, John Bogaert of the Bogaert Construction Co. of Essex, was engaged to handle the renovation.

On inspecting the barn, Bogaert found all the timbers sound except for some rot at the ends of posts that rested on the concrete floor of the lower level, where animals were once housed. These posts were easily repaired.

Bogaert also found that, while there had been no cows or horses in the barn for at least twenty years, there was still an accumulation of ancient manure in the manure shed. So the renovation began—as do so many barn renovations—with hauling away the old manure. The entire interior of the barn was then powerwashed with a solution of a mild household detergent and water to get rid of dust, grime, and all traces of manure.

The concrete floor on the first, or ground, level was broken up with

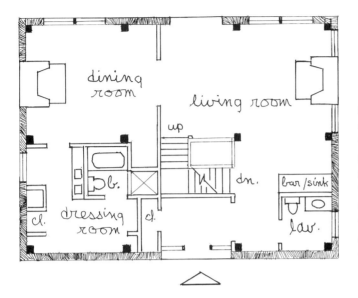

SECOND FLOOR: *Main entry is same size as the old barn doors that opened for hay wagons. It now leads past stairway into living room. Both living room and dining room have fireplaces that were added when barn was renovated. Bar sink built into living room wall includes a microwave oven—handy for heating dishes to be served in the adjacent dining room. (Illustration by Mary Lohmann.)*

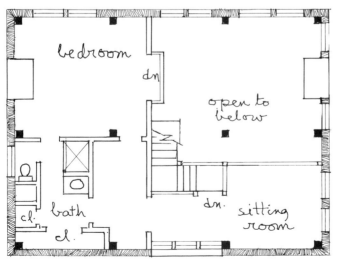

THIRD FLOOR: *Sitting room and stair landing overlook living room, which is open to roof. Bathrooms on third and second floors line up with each other to simplify plumbing installation. (Illustration by Mary Lohmann.)*

a jackhammer so that the six old cow stanchions could be removed, and since there was no cellar, a floor drain was installed before a new concrete floor was poured. The area is now the kitchen and family dining room. The old manure shed is used as an occasional guest room/den.

The original siding was left in place. The age-mellowed wood on the inside face of the siding makes handsome interior paneling.

In order to insulate the outside walls, 2-by-3 furring was installed over the old exterior siding. Rigid foam insulation was installed between the furring strips and the entire wall surface was covered with an air infiltration barrier followed by tongue-and-groove siding painted a driftwood gray.

The same idea was used on the roof: first came the application of insulating sheathing, and then new wood shingles were added. This allowed the roof boards and rafters on the interior to be left exposed.

Since being cleaned of accumulated dust and grime, the chestnut timbers, now burnished and glowing, needed no additional stain or sealer. Old wood was also used as mantels and surrounds for the two fireplaces installed as part of the renovation, one in the living room on the second level and one in the dining room. Baseboard hot-water heat was chosen as unobtrusive and practical, and a ceiling fan was installed in the living room to force downward the warm air that accumulates at this point.

It should please architect Floyd to learn that several old-time residents of the area were not aware that the old barn had been renovated. "You must be kidding," one of them said to us when we mentioned we were going to photograph the barn for this book. "Why, I drive past that old barn maybe two or three times a month and it looks the same as it did when I was a kid and used to play in the field right in front of it."

THE TOWNSEND MOORES

"The only way we could entertain was to put our friends to work."

———⟨∞⟩———

In 1946, just after World War II, housing of any kind was hard to come by, and the young Townsend Moores needed a place to live and start a family. What they found was an old stone-and-frame bank barn in Darlington, Pennsylvania, about thirty miles from Philadelphia. The barn with six acres of gently rolling farmland was $3,000.

Built around 1850, the 30-by-52-foot cow-and-hay barn was in pretty good shape, with the exception of the roof. Bubbles Moore says the first time they saw it, "the sun was shining through holes in the roof, and all the leftover grain, mostly oats, had sprouted and was growing inside." Rain that had come through the gaping holes had obviously assisted in this indoor garden display. Townie says the roof was not completely shot, since the timbers had not yet begun to rot, despite the leaks. "We caught it just in time," he says. "Another year or so and the timbers would have been well on the road to decay."

With the roof so obviously the first order of business, Bubbles and Townie started ripping off the old shingles and roof boards immediately upon taking possession of the property. Then came the job of installing new sheathing and new shingles. Townie had begun commuting to his office in Philadelphia, so Bubbles spent many days on the roof, hard at work with hammer and nails. Finally, it was finished, and she felt a real sense of accomplishment. But the day after it was finished, a hard rain came and they discovered that the roof was leaking badly. "I was in tears," she recalls. "It was heartbreaking. I knew we must have done something terribly wrong." As it turned out, they hadn't closed up one wall properly, but it was not a serious mistake and was easily fixed. Much to her relief.

Now that the roof was done, they could begin the business of planning just how they wanted to renovate. The first two levels of the barn were native fieldstone two feet thick; the third level and the attic were wood frame. Since they didn't want to do anything that would destroy the essential character of the barn, they had an architect draw up some plans, which cost them $75, a goodly sum in those days. But the plans didn't

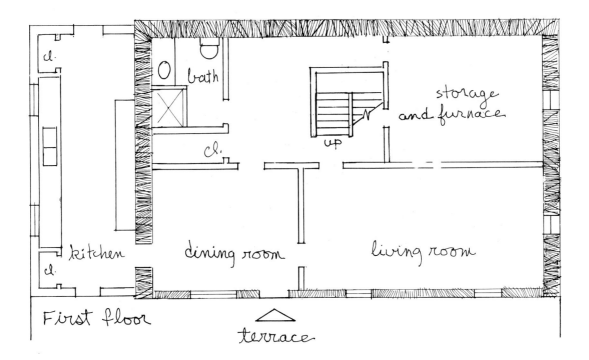

cl.

bath

storage
and furnace

cl.

up

kitchen

cl.

dining room

living room

cl.

First floor

terrace

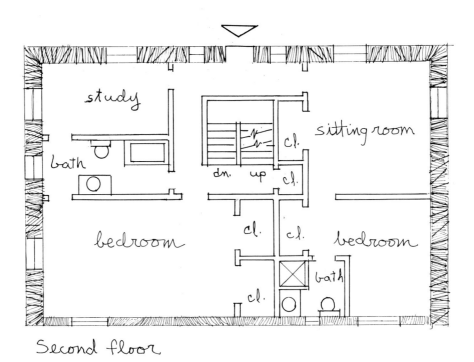

study

sitting room

bath

cl.

dn.   up

cl.

bedroom

cl.   cl.

bedroom

cl.

bath

cl.

Second floor

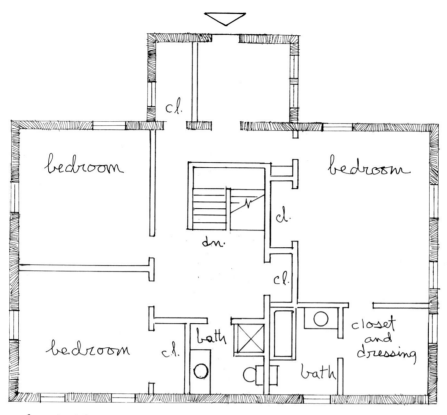

cl.

bedroom

bedroom

dn.

cl.

cl.

bedroom

cl.

bath

closet
and
dressing

bath

Third floor

FIRST FLOOR: *Entry is from brick-paved terrace into dining room. The 12-by-30-foot kitchen was added onto west wall. Shaded outlines shown in plan indicate original stone walls. The family lived on this level for five years while upper floors were being renovated.*

SECOND FLOOR: *Door under ramp is outside entry to this level. Door on south side in master bedroom leads to the large covered porch, which also shelters terrace below. Bathroom connects to master bedroom and study. Sitting room connects to entry hall, bedroom, and bath.*

THIRD FLOOR: *Stone-sided ramp leads to entry door set into vestibule on this floor. Stairs, two bedrooms, occupy space where wagons once discharged their loads of grain and hay. This floor and attic have wood frame exterior walls. North, east, and west walls on lower level are of stone. (Illustrations by Mary Lohmann.)*

seem right for them, so they decided to trust their own judgment and work it out for themselves.

They had a lot to do, and not much money, so they had to do things piecemeal. The plan was to set up temporary living quarters on the first floor—the grade level—where the animals had once been housed. Bubbles says there were "two standing horse stalls and the rest was for cows." The old, hardened manure would have to be removed first, so with pick and shovel, they set to work. Almost immediately, her shovel struck something hard. "Hey," she called to her husband, "this sounds solid." Turned out it was—a concrete floor in good condition. "Saved us a heck of a lot of money," says Bubbles.

After thoroughly cleaning and washing down the entire first floor, including brushing and oiling the posts and beams, they had electricity and water brought in by professionals and set up a temporary kitchen and a bathroom. Some months later, they moved in. They would live in these temporary quarters for five years while the renovations were going on. During this time they became a real family—with two children, a dog, and a cat. The children slept on bunk beds in temporarily partitioned-off bedrooms, and their parents made do with an equally small space. The living room was then only 7 feet by 15 feet, Bubbles told us, "and the only way we could entertain was to put our friends to work. But," she added, "we had some fine parties." When child number three arrived, the upstairs was finished off enough so that they could move into more roomy quarters on the second floor.

All the major work was contracted out, but there was still plenty to do. They had decided to utilize the three existing levels as they were originally framed wherever possible. All timbers were to be left exposed— both posts and ceiling beams. Unlike most renovators today, they had no wish to have double-height, open ceilings, so the ceilings in all the rooms are fairly low, looking very Early American. The walls and the ceilings in between the timbers in all rooms were drywalled or plastered, and painted white, a nice counterpoint to the old timbers.

Structural changes included the removal of the entire wood-framed south wall. This created a broad, sheltered terrace off the living and dining rooms and, on the second floor, a covered porch they planned to use as an outdoor sleeping area in summer. They also had a 12-by-30-foot stick-built kitchen addition put on the west side, next to the dining room. A fieldstone fireplace was added in the dining room.

In order to leave the stone exposed on the interior, they decided not to insulate the 24-inch-thick walls, but instead painted the end walls white in order to lighten both living room and dining room. The rear walls in both rooms were left in natural fieldstone. Townie says that they do sweat in hot humid weather, but "it's not a serious problem, so we just live with it." Books are kept on the upper levels, just in case of any mildew problem. According to Townie, the uninsulated stone walls have not had any real impact on their heating bills, since they close off the upper level in winter, unless their now-grown children or other guests are visiting. They heat with an oil-fired circulating-hot-water baseboard system and have a separate zone for the kitchen.

It took twenty years to complete the renovation exactly as they wanted it, since, as Townie says, "financing is always a problem with a project of this sort, and we had to hold off on certain things until we had the money to pay for it."

Today, of course, the 5,000-square-foot renovation is complete. It includes five bedrooms, five baths, living and dining rooms, a study, a sitting room, and a kitchen. The attic has been left unfinished, and there one can see the complex roof framing—the rafters, purlins, braces, and struts, all mortised and tenoned—just as they were framed 140 years ago.

Because the renovation took place over such a long period, the Moores can only estimate the total cost, but believe it to be "somewhere between $80,000 and $100,000."

Townie is now retired and devotes as much time as he wishes to his avocation—fine cabinet work. Several pieces of his furniture are used throughout the house—exquisite examples of eighteenth-century cabinetry by a twentieth-century expert. Bubbles is an active member of the local garden club and, in addition to her work there, has put in, and maintained, all the landscaping and the flower gardens that surround the barn house and that are lovely indeed.

In June of 1990, photographer Tom Hopkins and his assistant, Paul Liu, visited the Moores to photograph their house for this book. Bubbles and Townie insisted they stay for dinner and also that they stay the night. Tom says, "Not only that, they served us a wonderful breakfast." The two visitors had a delightful time, enjoying good company and lots of good food in this comfortable and attractive renovated barn house.

Snack area is complete with microwave, refrigerator, and facilities for light meals. On left, past painted wooden folk art figure made by local artist, is a separate bedroom, which can be closed off with sliding pocket doors concealed in walls. Blue-and-white half-curtains are on Dutch doors in bedroom, which can be opened for through ventilation with doors in the living room. (Photo by Eberhard Luethke.)

THE LUTESES' BARN

" . . . a stone's throw in either direction to the water."

———◦∞◦———

Dr. and Mrs. Chris Lutes needed a barn—not for horses, cows, or hay, but as a place to store "the tremendous amount of stuff" their five children, now all in their twenties, had been bringing home for years. This vast accumulation had begun to overflow the Luteses' winter home in Portland, Maine, so they decided that a barn would be just the place to put it all. They would build the barn at their summer place in a seacoast community not far from Portland, which Harriet Lutes describes as wonderfully undisturbed by modern development, a peaceful place, "like stepping back in time."

Chris Lutes, a cardiac surgeon, had always been interested in post-and-beam construction, and had seen an ad in a magazine advertising "Houses & Barns, by John Libby, est. 1971." The company, Barn Masters, Inc., happened to be in Freeport, not far from Portland, so he went over one day to meet Libby and observe the operation of the workshop. Watching the careful cutting of the large posts and beams and the detailing of the interlocking joints, Chris was impressed. Besides building new timber frame houses and barns, Libby had also been in the business of restoring historic buildings since the early seventies. There was no question that he and his staff were interested, knowledgeable, and knew what they were doing. They seemed just the right people to build the new barn.

Harriet and Chris knew what they wanted. It had to be attractive, since it was only a hundred or so feet from the main house, a big, old-fashioned beach cottage, only "a stone's throw from the water in either direction." It had to be sturdy, and have plenty of storage space, and be large enough to include a guest apartment on the upper level. It also had to blend in with the general architecture of this Downeast, 1920s-style community.

Getting together with Barn Masters's design and architectural staff, the Lutes soon saw their ideas translated into a workable plan for a 24-by-36-foot, two-story, classic New England barn with a cupola for ventilation and light and a small balcony overlooking the grounds and the main house.

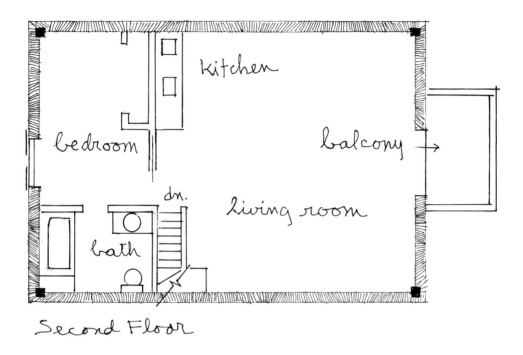

Second Floor

SECOND FLOOR: *Spacious living/dining room has small kitchen/snack area. French pocket doors separate bedroom from living area. Leading out to the 6-by-10 balcony are French doors that let in plenty of light. At bedroom end, Dutch doors and roof skylight bring in additional natural light. Apartment is a roomy 864 square feet. (Illustration by Mary Lohmann.)*

FIRST FLOOR: *Garage and storage floor, originally concrete, is now attractively bricked over. A slate potting sink (not shown) in corner by windows is handy to gardens. (Illustration by Mary Lohmann.)*

The guest apartment would have a living room, bedroom, bath, and a small space for casual meals.

As soon as the plans were approved, Libby's shop began making up the timbers for the frame. Each post, beam, and rafter was cut to exact size, each mortise and tenon checked to fit perfectly together. A protective coating of tung oil was the finishing touch to keep the timbers from absorbing stains and dirt during shipping and handling.

Once the foundation was in, Libby's crew erected the frame, assembled with wood pegs, in only one day. The rest of the work—siding, roofing, wiring, plumbing, and installation of the upstairs living quarters— would be handled by the contractors Libby had worked with before and could recommend.

A concrete floor was poured on the ground level to make it suitable for use as storage space—or as a garage, if needed. (Later, the Luteses, after a trip to Winterthur, the du Pont museum of beautiful gardens, fine furniture, and American decorative arts near Wilmington, added a brick floor over the concrete—a nice touch.) Stairs leading to the second level

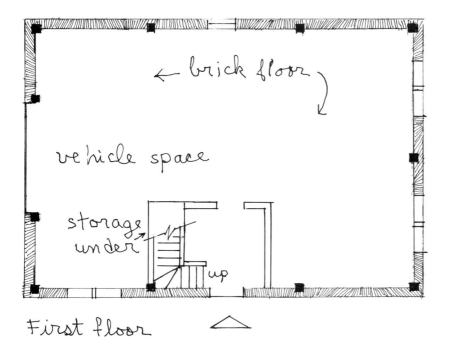

First floor

were installed. The 864-square-foot space on the second level is a spacious, light-filled apartment with a large living room, now attractively and comfortably furnished with chintz-covered love seats and a large sofa. There is even room for a small baby grand piano. A snack area is fitted into one corner, complete with table and chairs, a microwave, and a small refrigerator.

The bedroom and bath are separated from the living area by sliding doors that fit into pockets in the partitioning wall. Glass-arched French doors allow plenty of natural light into the living room and lead to the little 6-by-10-foot balcony overlooking the grounds and the main house, just a hundred or so feet away. In the bedroom, Dutch doors on the long wall add more natural light; and in the bathroom, a skylight is used for light and ventilation. Electric baseboard heat keeps the place cozy whenever warmth is needed.

Harriet Lutes, who designates herself as a "former professional volunteer," was also, for some fourteen years, a consulting chemist to a large camera company, and commuted to the Boston area until their fifth child was born. Now, the visual arts, especially dance, are her main interests. She and Chris are crazy about the barn. Says Harriet Lutes, "It is the place we escape to when things become too frantic at the house." Even when things are not all that frantic, they stay in the barn "as much as possible." Since it is thoroughly insulated, they can come out even in the winter, if they wish. And, as their children marry and grandchildren begin to arrive, Harriet says, they plan to "render the main house unto the children" and relax in the beauty and serenity of their barn house.

The broad, horizontal lines of this newly constructed post-and-beam house make it seem very much larger than it actually is, while at the same time giving it a "settled" look, as though it had been there for a very long time. The wide roof overhang and the pergola shade the house comfortably from the California sun. (Photo by Kasparowitz, Architectural Photography.)

SUE AND JOEL FARLEY

" . . . played with floor plans for a long time."

———— ⌾ ————

The little one-story post-and-beam timber frame house that Sue and Joel Farley had built in Paso Robles, California, in 1987 is not, in the strict sense of the term, a barn house. It has exposed timbers and a ceiling open to the roof peak. But according to Terry Turney, head of Pacific Post and Beam, the company in San Luis Obispo that constructed the house, "coach house" is probably a more apt term, since it is reminiscent of those built around the turn of the century in the Craftsman style. The timber details—hand cut and wood pegged—were also strongly influenced by Charles and Henry Greene, architects of Southern California who, in the first quarter of the century, became famous for their interpretation of the bungalow—until that time a favorite style of the British Arts and Crafts movement and, earlier still, popular in British India. With its horizontal lines, shaded porch, and low pitched roof, the house has much in common

The tongue-and-groove fir ceiling rises to a 13-foot peak, giving a huge lift to this "one big room built around a core." The fine craftsmanship of the timber frame is evident in every detail. (Photo by Kasparowitz, Architectural Photography.)

with the bungalow, yet is uniquely itself because of the Farley's individual requirements.

We include the house because the interior, with its exposed and beautifully constructed timber frame of quality Douglas fir, is very barnlike. We also think it is an excellent example of how comfortable and roomy a one-floor, open-plan house can be if it is well designed and well executed. Interior living space in the house totals 864 square feet, but with an 8-by-36-foot covered porch outside, there is a grand total of 1,152 square feet for both indoor and outdoor activities. The house is set on rolling pastureland dotted with groves of California oak growing in low patches amid the eighty acres of land the Farleys own. A 4-foot overhang and a pergola block the summer sun and keep the house comfortable in hot weather.

The Farleys do not only live in the house; Joel, a computer software consultant, also has office space there. Sue, who works with him, has her office in a 26-foot-long trailer not far from the house. They lived in the trailer while construction was going on. The Farleys started C-Ware Corporation, their computer software company, about eight years ago, and according to Sue, "to our surprise, were suddenly successful with the product." They had been renting an apartment in Paso Robles, but with success staring them in the face, needed permanent quarters rather quickly.

Sue says they "played with floor plans for a long time" and had at first planned to build a sort of guest house, then a larger house later. But now, they are so busy with their business, and this house is working out so well, that other building plans are on hold for the time being.

The Farleys applied for a building permit in January and moved in about six months later, in June. Pacific Post and Beam hand-cut the timbers for the house in their beamery in San Luis Obispo, erected the frame, and put in windows, doorframes, and floors. Since not all electricians are familiar with or like to work with stress-skin panels, with which the house is insulated, PP&B also did the wiring and built the pergola outside. The Farleys did most of the interior finish work themselves—drywall, taping, painting, installing kitchen cabinets and tile counters, and all the myriad details that are part of making a home.

The living and sleeping areas of the house are built around a utility core, which includes a convenient Pullman kitchen, a full bathroom with a built-in electric heater, and a wood stove in the living room to take the chill off the sometimes cool California nights. There is a laundry at the kitchen end of the core, and, in the sleeping area, two 6-foot walk-in

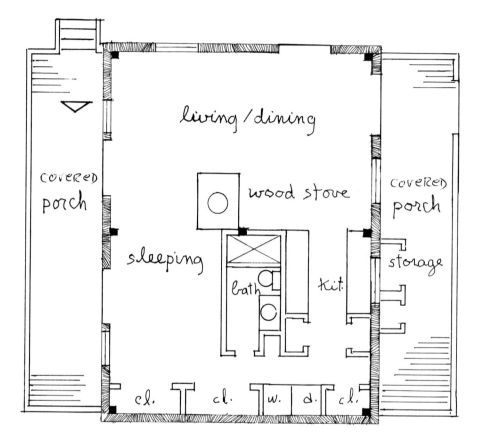

ONE-FLOOR HOUSE: *864 square feet of well-planned space. Entry is from the covered porch via two pairs of French doors; one pair opens into the living/dining room, the other into the sleeping area. Kitchen, bath, and laundry are in one efficient central core, leaving the major portion of space uncluttered. Wood stove is placed so as to provide warmth to both living/dining and sleeping area. Note outside storage areas off kitchen and closets on each side of washer/dryer on rear wall. (Illustration by Mary Lohmann.)*

closets. The house is very light, with many windows and two pairs of French doors, one pair opening into the living area from the porch, the other pair opening into the sleeping area. Partway through the building process, they decided to put two skylights in the roof over the kitchen. This was done by PP&B.

Sue says they had a nasty surprise one night shortly after they moved in. They were sleeping soundly, when suddenly they were awakened by a loud "thud and a piercing screech" from the kitchen. Rushing in, they found that one of their cats had fallen thirteen feet through the new skylight. (Being a cat, he was unhurt, and still had eight other lives to spare.) Even though the skylights were screened, the cat had apparently jumped on the screen hard enough to break through. Now the last thing they do before retiring is close the skylights.

The house is attractively furnished with antiques they brought with them from Rochester, New York, and which seem very much at home in the California sunshine. The effect is simple and charming, and the exposed posts and beams invite close inspection of the skilled joinery techniques used in assembling the frame, which was—a nice touch—erected by the same craftsman who cut the joints at the beamery.

Front view of barn when old roofing was being stripped and siding removed. Concrete block for much-discussed chimney was laid in place. It would later be faced. Note how in old barns wood louvers were used for ventilation. The Petersons would later replace these with glass windows. (Photo by Jonah Peterson.)

JONAH AND BEVERLY PETERSON

*". . . a blend of a lot of people's ideas . . . or just stored
in my head."*

———— ∞ ————

More than a hundred years of family history make Jonah and Beverly
Peterson's renovated bank barn in Delphi, Indiana, a very special place.

According to marks on some of the timbers, Jonah's grandfather built
the barn in 1886, on his sixty-acre farm. He had bought this particular
acreage because it was close to a schoolhouse and he wanted his children
to have a better education than he received as a boy.

The Petersons were living in Chicago and Jonah, a business analyst,
was thinking of retiring. His mother, anxious for Jonah and Beverly to
come back to Indiana, offered them the old barn, plus twenty acres. They
accepted her offer.

After leaving Chicago, they moved into a mobile home on the property
in Delphi while they considered their options—whether to renovate the
barn where Jonah as a boy had milked cows, pitched hay, and done other
farm chores, or to build a new house. They finally decided to use as much
of the barn as possible and "go on from there."

On close inspection Jonah found that the oak beams—hand-hewn
and a century old—were as sound as they were the day the barn was built.
So the focus of the interior design was to leave exposed as many of these
old timbers as possible.

"There was never any formal plan for remodeling the barn," Jonah
says. "It was a blend of a lot of people's ideas, written on matchbooks and
napkins or just stored in my head." Gradually an overall plan emerged,
one that divided the barn into four levels totaling 4,400 square feet. This
would be more than ample for a four-bedroom, four-bath house.

The location of the chimney was a major design hang-up. Family
and friends had different ideas as to where it should be located. A center
chimney was the most obvious, but it would break up the open expanse
of the living room created by the 23½-foot-high ceiling. It was finally
decided to build the chimney in a corner, where it would not detract from
the space of the living/dining area.

Renovation work began in early 1985. Jonah worked along with the

After three and a half years, the renovation was complete. Barn house is same height as original barn, but by grading earth around it, renovated barn appears less tall than it actually is. (Photo by Kasco Mfg. Co.)

Jonah prepared to use "The Saw"—the indispensable tool— to square a log from which boards would be made. (Photo by Kasco Mfg. Co.)

carpenter, Vern Criswell, and got occasional help from his brother, Morris, and brother-in-law, Stanley Wolven.

All the old roofing and siding would have to be removed and replaced, and Jonah, even after many inquiries, couldn't find any good suggestions on how to insulate and still leave the old timbers exposed on the interior. He finally found the solution in a book, *Alex Wade's Guide to Affordable Houses*, that described how to build insulating panels similar to the stress-skin panels sold commercially today. He asked several lumberyards to make up the panels for him, but none were interested. One, however, said that if he would buy the materials—waferboard and rigid foam insulation—from them and make up the panels himself, they would store the completed panels, which would be bulky, until they were ready to be installed.

Jonah accepted this arrangement, ordered the materials, and soon "the whole place was cluttered up with sheets of waferboard and rigid foam." With some help, he assembled the panels and shipped them to the lumberyard to be stored until needed.

By May of 1985 all of the panels had been installed, along with new roofing, siding, and electric wiring, which Jonah did himself. A well had been drilled, a septic system installed, and the telephone was in. By the

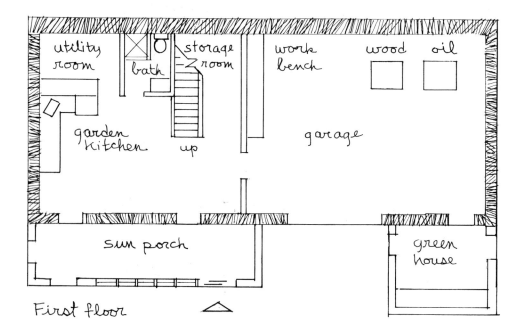

First floor

(Top left) FIRST FLOOR (GRADE LEVEL): *Sun porch and greenhouse additions flank entry from outside into garden kitchen and garage. Entry is sheltered by deck on level above. Half bath and utility room are convenient to kitchen used for canning, preserving, and preparation of meals too large for the second-floor kitchen to handle. Combination workshop/furnace area includes central air conditioner and two furnaces; one wood-burning, the other oil-fired.*

(Top right) SECOND FLOOR (MAIN LEVEL): *Main entry is from sheltered deck leading into living/dining area. Stairs between living and dining areas lead down to grade level, those by kitchen/dinette up to library. Stairs by master bedroom lead to third-floor bedrooms. Living/dining area is open to above.*

(Bottom left and right) THIRD FLOOR: *Each bedroom has access to shared bath, stairs, and the balcony, which overlook living/dining area. Also on third floor is 15-by-20-foot library set over kitchen, overlooking living room but not accessible from bedrooms.*

(Bottom far right) FOURTH FLOOR: *Open loft above bedrooms on third floor can be used as bedroom, if needed. It, too, overlooks living room. (Illustrations by Mary Lohmann.)*

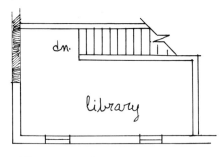

Third floor

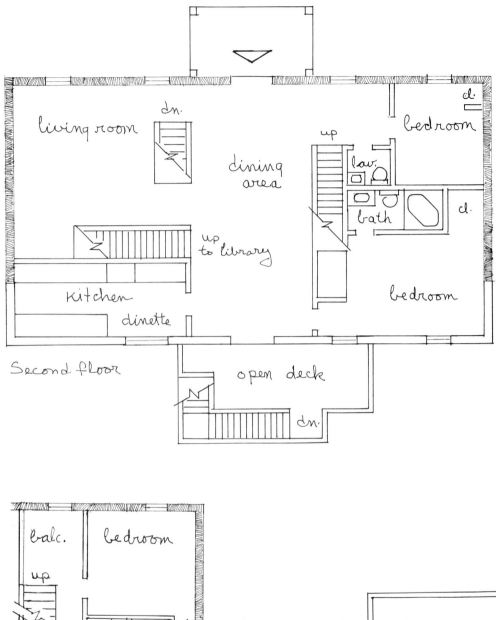

living room

dn.

dining area

up

bedroom

cl.

lav.

bath

cl.

bedroom

up to library

Kitchen

dinette

Second floor

open deck

dn.

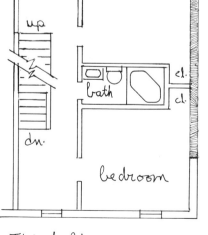

balc.

bedroom

up

bath

cl.

cl.

dn.

bedroom

Third floor

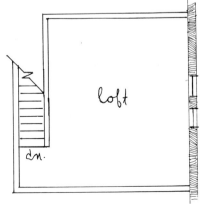

loft

dn.

Fourth floor

following year there was a ground-level kitchen, and two furnaces had been put in—one oil fired, the other wood burning.

The woodlots on the farm contained many fine trees—red and white oak, sycamore, locust, walnut, cherry, and maple. Jonah decided that most of the lumber he needed for interior work—framing, trim, staircases, and banisters—could come from his own trees. At a friend's suggestion, he invested in a band saw. Made by the Kasco Manufacturing Company, The Saw, as it is called, could handle logs up to 24 feet in diameter and 14 feet long. This became the "indispensable tool" that enabled him to first square a log, then, by adjusting the log rest, cut the log into boards of any size required. All this with minimum effort on his part. One 18-inch-square log 14 feet long could yield 430 board feet of beautiful lumber. All agreed that the investment had been well worth the money, not only because it was efficient but because of the pleasure the entire family took in knowing that all that beautiful wood came from their own land. Boards that were to be used for interior trim were run through a planer, then stained and given a coat of varnish by Beverly. Jonah would have preferred to have allowed the wood to season but was pushed for time. However,

this did not seem to create a serious problem. "I used a lot of it for rough framing where it wouldn't matter if the timbers shrunk a bit as they dried out," Jonah told us. "And on the trim I set each piece in such a way that any open seams that might occur would not be too obvious."

It took three and a half years to complete the renovation, but the barn house is now a spacious, comfortable home that includes on the rock-walled lower level a garden kitchen, a sun porch, a greenhouse, and a work/furnace/garage area. The lower level is surrounded on three sides by an earth berm.

On the second level is the living room/dining area, a smaller kitchen, the master bedroom and bath, a second bedroom, and a half bath. Upstairs on the third level are two more bedrooms and a bath, and on the fourth level is an open loft that overlooks the living room. There is also a small library above the kitchen. The wonderful variety of new woods used in the interior—sycamore, honey locust, ash, walnut, and more—augment and point up the antique timbers of the original barn frame. Beverly's collection of homemade quilts, used in decorating beds, banisters, and walls, adds just the right country touch to this completely unique home.

The Petersons financed their renovations from the proceeds of the sale of their Chicago house. Jonah figures the total cost was around $50,000 and thinks the place is now worth well over $200,000. But he and Beverly wouldn't sell it for the world. In fact, they're going to keep on fixin' up the place—the next project will be adding a fireplace.

Stairs, railings, and all new wood construction in the house, except for flooring and exterior siding, were made with lumber from Peterson's own trees. (Photo by Kasco Mfg. Co.)

View of entire complex from east cornfield. Large opening in center of building in foreground is vehicle drive-through to inner courtyard. Window to bedroom is in small dormer to left of cupola, which is 54 feet above ground level. (Photo by Janet A. Null, A.I.A.)

JENIFER AND FULLER COWLES

"It was a great experience, but I lost about a year from my work."

———⌁———

Jenifer and Fuller Cowles fell in love with the view from a dilapidated old barn set on a plain above the Saint Croix River in Minnesota. A favorite pastime, when they were visiting the Cowles family farmstead, was to stroll over to the old barn in the late afternoon, climb to an upper loft, and peering through gaps in the old siding, marvel at the beauty of the fields of ripening corn rippling in the end-of-day breeze. It would be wonderful to have a home here.

The old barn was too far gone to renovate, so it would have to be razed. They would build a new barn house on the old site and combine it with a studio where Fuller, a sculptor, could construct his larger-than-lifesize pieces. They would keep the silo, a tall, concrete structure that despite a missing roof was reassuringly solid. This would be a link with the past, a historical anchor.

Some months before in New England, the Cowles had visited friends who lived in a timber frame barn house built from a kit made by Timberpeg, a manufacturer of post-and-beam houses, in West Lebanon, New Hampshire. Fuller, skilled in working with wood himself, was impressed by the massive timbers and visible skill of the mortise-and-tenon joinery, which seemed so compatible with his own work.

Contacting Timberpeg, he found that they would indeed engineer and manufacture the frame for the projected studio/barn house, shipping it to Minnesota from one of Timberpeg's several out-of-state plants. Design consultation on the structural frame would also be included in their services. The architectural and spatial design would be the responsibility of the architect and the owner.

The Cowles decided to use Janet Null, a young architect in Troy, New York, whom they had known for years. Both Fuller Cowles and Janet Null had studied in Europe—Null on a fellowship in Rome and Fuller in Berlin. They shared similar tastes in art and in architecture and had much in common.

Janet Null had never worked with a manufactured post-and-beam

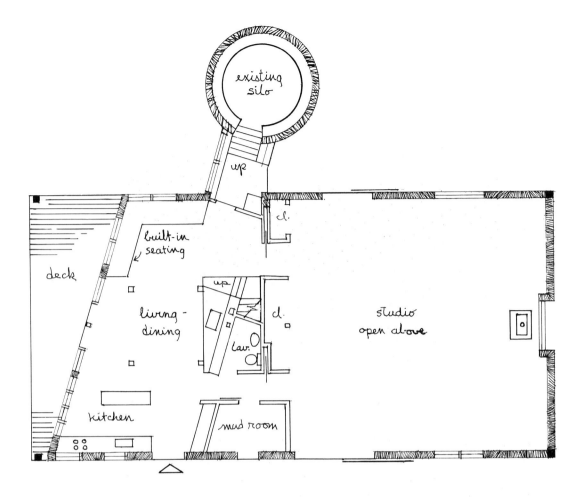

FIRST FLOOR: *Main entry from inner courtyard leads past kitchen into living/dining area, which can also be reached from studio or mudroom. This area, which has built-in seating along south and west walls, is connected by slate-paved walk to old silo. Living/dining area opens onto south-facing deck. South wall was cut at an angle to maximize solar heat gain. Heat is augmented by wood-burning stove on raised hearth, which is cut at same angle as wall. Freestanding chimney wall is wrapped at side and rear by stairs up to second level. Two-story-high studio is provided with ample natural light by skylights and glass areas on north, east, and west walls. Sliding barn-style doors allow entry of trucks delivering supplies for owner's large-size sculptures. (Illustration by Mary Lohmann.)*

building system before but found the project interesting and challenging. She says she enjoyed "working with a traditional and ancient building system in order to create contemporary spaces." Timberpeg's engineers were very cooperative in adapting their system to the unusual scale and configuration of the design, she said.

An essential element in the planning was to capture and reinvent

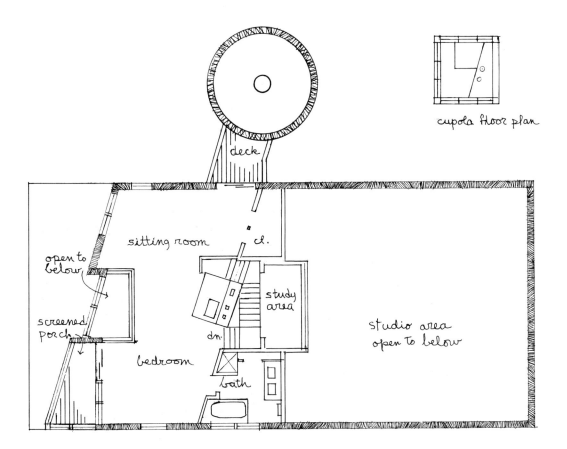

cupola floor plan

SECOND FLOOR: *Bedroom and sitting areas open to below and flow into one another, separated only by wood stove on raised hearth and by chimney wall. Bedroom opens onto screened porch. Entrance to study area—now used as mezzanine office by owner—is from stair landing. Stairs on this level wrap chimney wall as they descend to first floor. Wood deck leads from sitting room to silo. The 23-foot ladder in this area leads to a private retreat in the cupola. (Illustration by Mary Lohmann.)*

many of the qualities that Jenifer and Fuller had found so appealing in the old barn. This meant, of course, that the architect would have to visit the site—which she did—making the first of several trips to Minnesota. She, too, became captivated by the site and the idea of evoking the feeling—if not the actuality—of the older structure. This she accomplished in several ways.

The new building would have the same southerly orientation as the old one, and as existing buildings on the farm. In order to achieve as much solar heat gain as possible—which Fuller very much wanted to do—

161

the south wall would be cut at the optimum solar angle—an interesting and unusual departure from the traditional rectangular barn. This would leave a slice of space—a long, narrow triangle—that would result in a sort of pocket deck. A pleasant way to approach the south entrance.

Another departure from barn tradition would be a lavish use of glass on this south side, where several windows of different sizes and shapes, placed irregularly, would enable those inside to see the same lovely view that Jenifer and Fuller had enjoyed from the dim interior of the old barn.

A major element of the basic plan would be the 34-by-36-foot studio—an enormous two-story-high work space that would occupy over half the total square footage of the house. The height of the studio would establish the height of the house, which would be divided into two floors—the upper to be the private quarters, with bedroom, bath, sitting room, and study. Kitchen, dining, and living areas would all be downstairs. The rooms were not to be separated in the conventional manner by partitions, but would instead flow into one another, defined only by function and choice of furnishings. The absence of partitions would also allow a free flow of solar heat gain, which would be augmented by wood-burning stoves in the living/dining area, the upper bedroom level, and in the studio. Radiant electric heating coils in the concrete slab and supplemental electric fan-wall heaters would provide the backup heating system.

The plan also called for a barn-style cupola, which would be reached by a ladder. The studio would have large, barn-style doors, similar in size and design to the drive-through of the old barn so that instead of hay wagons, trucks could enter. A crane, which Fuller would use from time to time, was made an integral part of the building. It is supported on the two main glue-laminated beams of the studio roof. The old silo would be reroofed and a row of clerestory windows will encircle the new roof to bring in light from above. A hot tub has been built outdoors next to the silo.

When, after much deliberation and concentrated thought, the plans were made final, Timberpeg started the customizing of the timber frame. All post and beams were cut to exact measurements; mortises and tenons and pegs were all hand cut.

The frame arrived at the site in October, shortly after the foundations were in. A representative of Timberpeg was also on hand to supervise the erection. Fuller acted as his own general contractor and, with the able collaboration of Greg Alson, a fine local carpenter and contractor and his

South facade of house shows generous use of glass and unusual placement of windows. Front of this south wall is cut on the diagonal at optimal angle for solar heat gain, thus creating a narrow, triangular deck. (Photo by Janet A. Null, A.I.A.)

crew, it took about four weeks to erect the massive 34-by-72-foot structure. Although they had no special problems, it was hard and exacting work, and it was not until the following September that the barn house/studio was completed. It was a complex house to build and, as Fuller pointed out, "Winter is not the ideal time to build in this part of the country. I worked along with the carpenters and it was a great experience, but I lost about a year from my work."

At the center of the first-floor living area, symbolizing the basic scheme of the architectural concept and meant for gathering 'round, is a raised hearth with a wood-burning stove. Here, towering above the stove, is a freestanding chimney wall of monumental size rising behemothlike through the entire house. The wall is faced with hundreds of glazed, hand-crafted tiles, created by Fuller Cowles, in a myriad of patterns and colors, interspaced with a three-dimensional collage of various "found" objects, some mundane, others fanciful—a truly extraordinary work. Running straight up through the bedroom/sitting area, the wall culminates in the cupola, which is reached by a 23-foot-high ladder. Of butternut and black walnut and inlaid with images made from some more exotic woods, the ladder was constructed in the studio and brought in by the studio crane through Fuller's connecting mezzanine office. The cupola, which rises 54 feet above ground level, is—like the silo—a place of retreat. The views from that height are spectacular and, Fuller says, it is "a fine place to watch thunderstorms moving across the land."

CHAPTER SEVEN

If You Have to Move a Barn

Old barns are not always where they're wanted, so it's common practice to move them to another site. Depending on the barn, the entire structure can be moved or it can be dismantled and reassembled on a new site. Which method is best depends on the size of the barn, its condition, and the distance it must be moved. And, of course, the cost.

Move the Entire Barn

This can be a practical approach if the barn is in fairly good condition—sound timbers, siding and roofing worth saving—if the distance it will be moved is not too great, and if there are few, if any, obstacles to be overcome. The Johnsons in Colorado, for example, had to cut off the top half of their balloon-frame barn so it would fit under a highway overpass. Ed and Jane Dadey in Nebraska, on the other hand, moved five barns—all stud-built—from nearby farmsteads with relative ease. They did use professional house movers, however.

Moving the entire barn onto another site on the same property is the simplest and most cost-conserving situation. If the barn has to be moved along a main road, you have to be concerned with not only underpasses, but more important, with electric power lines. It can cost from $200 to $800 or more to remove each power line the barn must pass under. You would also need the help of local police to reroute traffic during the move, and this can be costly. An experienced house mover can judge whether it is feasible to go to this expense.

Even if the move is only a few feet, it takes careful preparation. The structure must be carefully braced so it will hold its shape and so timbers and joints will not be damaged during the move. It can cost from $5,000 to $10,000 just to prepare a timber frame barn for a move, depending on its condition and on the region of the country you are in.

After the barn has been securely braced, it is jacked up and set on rollers or wheels and is hauled by truck or tractor to the new site. An experienced barn mover in the Northeast quoted us a price of from $12,000 to $13,000 to move a post-and-beam barn a few hundred yards on the same property. Prices will vary according to region.

The barn will need new foundations, and these can run around $90 a linear, or running, foot. Because the barn frame may not be true, some movers suggest that the foundations be installed after the barn has been moved to the new site. Plumb lines are then dropped from each corner to provide accurate guides for the new foundations.

Look in the yellow pages under "House Movers," and choose one who has experience with barns. If you have a post-and-beam barn, you want a mover who has experience with this type of barn, because it is more difficult to move than a stud-built barn.

After the house mover has inspected the barn and looked over the route of the move, he can give you an estimate of the total cost, including preparation, the move itself, and the new foundations.

(Top) Antique New England barn prior to being dismantled. Note cupola. (Bottom) Frame stripped and ready to be dismantled with help of crane. (Photos by The Barn People.)

Dismantle the Barn

This has become the most common way to move a barn. Many old post-and-beam timber frame barns on abandoned farmsteads in the Northeast and elsewhere have been moved hundreds of miles in this fashion. John O'Brien's barn house, for example, was trucked from its original site in New Jersey to his building site in Maryland.

Aside from the fact that a dismantled barn can be hauled anywhere— if you are willing to pay the trucking cost—there are other advantages. One is that if some of the timbers are in poor condition they can be repaired or replaced with new timbers of similar size for less money than if the work were done on a standing barn. Also, only the elements you will actually use are moved. The worn-out roofing, rotted sills, flooring, and so forth can go directly to the nearest solid-waste dump.

Dismantling a timber frame barn is no job for the do-it-yourselfer. It is not only hard and exacting work but can be dangerous, and even if you don't get hurt in the process, you could do serious damage to some of the timbers or wood joints. Also, it takes a good deal of special equipment— for example: scaffolding, come-alongs, block and tackle, crane with operator, power drills for removing stubborn pegs. Play it smart and let an expert dismantle the barn and then re-erect the frame on your building site.

Try the yellow pages under "Builders-Restoration" for professional help. Local historical societies, residential architects and designers, real estate brokers, and local building inspectors may also give you leads, as may lumberyards.

Once you locate the right person, talk price right away. Dismantling an old barn and re-erecting the frame is highly labor-intensive work. It can take an experienced crew two to four weeks to take the old barn apart, mark each timber for ready assembly, clean and fumigate the timbers, remove all debris from the old site, then truck the frame to the new site. This can run $20,000 or more, depending on mileage to be covered. Re-erecting the frame is sometimes included in the estimate, but much depends on whether the builder or restorationist will go on to complete the whole house. Also, as with everything else, price depends on the region of the country you'll be living in.

Repairing cupola on ground. (Photo by The Barn People.)

Washing timbers to remove dirt and insects during repair process. (Photo by the Barn People.)

Replacing rotten tenon on a beam. (Photo by The Barn People.*)*

Epoxy adhesive secures new piece into rotted beam. (Photo by The Barn People.*)*

Restored bent laid out in shop. (Photo by The Barn People.)

A purlin system being hoisted into position by crane. (Photo by The Barn People.)

Now—having said all of the above, we feel obligated to tell you that tyros have in the past—and no doubt will continue—to dismantle old barns without professional help. In fact, we know of two rugged young women, Leslie Bracker and Monique Van de Ven in Woodstock, Vermont, who, just last summer, took down an old barn that was in the path of a highway-widening project. They even devised a way to remove the old slates from the roof without breaking any (well, maybe they broke a few). They did, however, hire a crane with operator to handle the rafters and other heavy timbers and they had additional assistance from a young man who works for them in their professional painting business. Also, both of these women had training in cabinetmaking and in woodworking. So they were certainly not unskilled.

Therefore, it really is up to you to decide if—despite our words of wisdom and warning—you want to go ahead and move or dismantle a barn yourself. If you do, just make sure you have the talent, the strength, allied skills and experience of some sort, and a basic understanding of how things—especially barns—are put together.

CHAPTER EIGHT

Planning
Your Barn House

W hether you are going to renovate, start anew with an old barn frame, or build from scratch, you'll need plans. You will need them to get a construction loan or mortgage, a building permit, reliable estimates for labor and materials, and, finally, to serve as a guide for those who will be doing the work—the general contractor, carpenter, plumber, and so on (or, if you are the main labor source, yourself).

Types of Plans

If you have built a house before or are familiar with house plans—often referred to as "blueprints" (because the sensitized paper used to make copies of the original drawings has a bluish tint)—you'll probably skip this part, but if you're new to the house game, better read on.

A set of plans can include five separate drawings—floor plan, elevations, sections, details, and site plan.

The *floor plan* is the most important of all. It gives the overall dimensions of the house and shows how the interior space is arranged—room dimensions; size and location of doors, windows, stairs, fireplaces, etc. Many old barns have been renovated and financed just on the basis of a floor plan.

Elevations detail the height of each side of the structure, show the size and location of windows and exterior doors, detail the eaves, give the height of the chimney above the roof, and specify other elements of the house that do not show on the floor plan.

Section drawings show a cross-section taken through one portion of the house; for example, the fireplace and chimney from base to roof and the manner in which framing is set around the chimney.

Detail drawings explain how a specific item—staircase, balcony, loft fireplace, and so forth—should be built.

The *site plan* shows the relation of the house to the lot, main road, and adjoining structures; and gives the location of the septic system, the well, and other features. A site plan can be important if you need to apply for a variance or to show the building department where the septic system will be in relation to the house and well.

Where to Get Plans

Firms that make and sell barn-style houses in a complete package or in a post-and-beam kit usually provide a floor plan and elevations—the basic plans. In addition, many of these firms have design staffs, using sophisticated computer-assisted design (CAD), who are ready, willing, and able to work with you or your architect to modify their basic plans to suit your particular needs. The design staff at Yankee Barn Homes, for example, custom-designed Paula Landesmann's vacation house to her exact requirements, as did Habitat/American Barn for the Bloom-Gwillim barn house and Timberpeg for the Cowles barn house/studio.

If you have had a timber framer/builder dismantle and re-erect your old barn frame, he or members of his firm will assist you in drawing up your plans. An additional plus in working with a timberwright is the scale model of your frame that he will construct for $100 or so. This three-dimensional model is an enormous help in planning the best use of interior space. If you plan to have two or more levels in your barn house, the timberwright's input will be invaluable in calculating stresses and strains on the main timbers.

The challenge in designing a barn house is how to divide the space to suit the demands of contemporary living while at the same time maintaining the feeling of openness that is so attractive in a barn. It is the exposed timbers—the revealed structure—that give a barn house its distinctive character, and the right architect or architectural designer can help you achieve this goal—a comfortable house with a "barn" feeling.

Look in the yellow pages under "Architects" and "Designers-Architectural" for design assistance. If the professional you call does not do barn houses, he or she may suggest a colleague who does. Word of mouth, of course, is often the best way to find the right person, especially if a friend has had experience with a particular architect or designer. Local building officials can give you names, but probably won't recommend one over another. Your real estate broker would be more apt to give you a personal reaction.

Many architects will work on an hourly basis, charging around $60 an hour and up, depending on the architect and the area. Some, however, will work only on a commission basis—15 to 20 percent of total construction costs. For this kind of money, the architect will plan your house, draw up materials and specification lists, recommend the general contractor, supervise construction, and be generally responsible for the whole project.

Architectural designers don't have the extensive training in all phases of construction—industrial and commercial as well as residential—that the registered architect must have, but they have studied at design schools and may have other training besides. Their hourly rate is a bit lower than the registered architect—around $40 to $50 an hour.

In searching for the right architect or designer, look for someone who has respect for barns and the way they are built—not all do. The professional timber framer/builder obviously loves to see open space framed with exposed timbers or else he would be in some other business. The individual you select to help plan your barn house should have a similar appreciation and also have experience renovating barns or building new barn house projects. Ask to see photographs of, or actually visit, completed barn house projects. Also make sure you like each other and can talk in a relaxed and comfortable fashion.

Once you have found the right person, let them know right away how much you want to spend on the project. No one can intelligently plan a house unless he or she knows what the budget is going to be.

Do Your Homework

The more input you can give a planner, the better your chance of getting exactly the right house for you. Tell him or her how you and your family like to live and specify your particular interests. List favorite things and pet peeves, if you have any. You have probably been clipping from home magazines and newspapers for a long time, so you may already have a scrapbook. If not, try to clip some ideas from current publications. Even if they won't work in your particular house, they indicate things of interest to you.

You may already have some favorite books on home building, decorating, and architecture. If not, spend some time in your local library in those particular sections. Also, visit bookstores for new or classic books on houses or barns. Books on remodeling and renovation can be of tremendous help. (See bibliography for recommended reading.)

Make up some rough floor plans showing how you visualize the layout of your barn house. The drawings might be a bit childlike, but the professional planner will get the idea.

Newly restored exterior showing new front entrance flanked by original old barn doors. Shed-roof garage was reframed and skylights were set in roof. (Photo by Tom Hopkins.)

THE DISERIO STONE BANK BARN

Living room on right of entrance stretches 36½ feet, the entire width of barn to dining area. Stone wall in this room was left intact, other spaces were divided with drywall partitions. Fan keeps warm air circulating in cold weather. (Photo by Tom Hopkins.)

The Hanna barn house in its original form.

(Top right) Completed barn house as it is today. Deck, running the length of the building, was expanded twice from its original 16-foot length to its present 45 feet, and now includes a hot tub. Two glass atrium doors on left of kitchen lead to deck. This view, from south meadow, shows the variously shaped windows and the glass areas that have been added, but from the road, what you see is a very large classic barn, freshly painted barn-red with old wagon doors "X-ed" in white and very few small windows. (Bottom right) First-floor level is devoted to comfortable, relaxed living with its cheerful, antiques-and-wicker-furnished sun room and dining area, and its compact kitchen, open to the entire space. Ceiling boards are framed with original chestnut beams and are supported by a steel girder running the length of the room. Girder is boxed in with old planking, which also serves as a chaseway to conceal electric, TV, and telephone wires. Two lally columns supporting girder are similarly encased in the white vertical rectangle dividing dining area and kitchen. (Photos by Tom Hopkins.)

The interior of the Hanna barn house before work began.

THE HANNA BARN HOUSE

THE BLOOM-GWILLIM BARN HOUSE

(Top) Sheltered front entry to three-level, post-and-beam, custom-designed barn house by architect Jeffrey Linfert. Basic material for timber frame package kit was supplied by Habitat/ American Barn, custom-cut to order. (Bottom) View into living room from broad entry hall. Kids' wing is two steps down on left. Just past kitchen on right is glimpse of fireplace on west wall where there is a view up to the roof rafters. Straight ahead are the two 20-inch-diameter exposed heating ducts, painted a high-tech blue. (Photos by Tom Hopkins.)

THE LUTES BARN

(Top) Fitting perfectly into the old-time Downeast summer community where it was recently built, the Lutes barn—guest apartment, storage place, potting shed, and parents' hideaway—fulfills all its designated functions, often even in winter. The little balcony, the fanlight over the French doors, and the cupola all contribute to the very Victorian feeling of the barn. (Bottom) Bright, airy, spacious, all apply to the guest apartment, with its elegant honey-colored timber frame as much a part of the decor as the attractive furnishings. View straight ahead is of the main house. (Photos by Eberhard Luethke.)

It isn't hard to imagine John Wayne sitting on the front porch of this Western barn house, so reminiscent is it of earlier days. The low, broad roofline and covered porch, overlooking a lush meadow, shelter the house from late-day sun. A rear deck off the kitchen, facing east, runs the length of house (excluding the downstairs bedroom), allowing more space for outdoor living. (Photo by Michael Shopenn.)

THE FRANKEN BARN HOUSE

A plenitude of windows on different levels make this an extraordinarily light house. Antique German painted cupboard and grand piano are focal points at this end of the living room, handsomely framed by 8-by-8-inch wood-pegged hand-cut timbers. (Photo by Michael Shopenn.)

(Bottom left) Vaulted ceiling and window placed skylight-high create feeling of far more space than the actual 15-by-15½-foot dimensions of the upstairs room would imply. Low windows under eaves admit morning sun and give a bedside view of the weather. (Photo by Michael Shopenn.)

THE PEABODY BARN HOUSE

Nestled into the Vermont hills, this multilevel barn house has as its core a 30-by-38-foot antique barn frame. Multiple additions add up to over 8,000 square feet. Granite traprock facing on wall of basement level is patterned after "an old Shaker barn concept," says Bill Peabody. Coffee-brown metal "standing seam" roof tops the wood-shingled exterior. (Photo by Tom Hopkins.)

Looking down through antique timbers from railed balcony on second floor above dining room. Tall maple-framed casement windows bring natural light to the entire downstairs area. The kitchen, open to the dining room, has counter-height casement windows and a breakfast bar that does double duty as a serving counter. Door on left opens to outside deck. Below is a view of the living room. Flooring in both areas is Mexican tile. (Photos by Tom Hopkins.)

THE BUTLER BARN

(Top left) Completed barn house re-erected on new site. Old wagon doors are now metamorphosed into tall, arched glass doors that open to south side, now terraced and landscaped. Door at far left in shed addition is main entry to house. (Bottom left) Wide expanse of French doors brings outdoor light into studio/living area that is made luminous as the light is reflected back by white-painted floor and ceiling. (Top right) Wood-framed fireplace wall is itself an artist's composition as form is played against form, light against dark. Kitchen is partitioned from sitting space by open shelves high enough to screen cooking procedures yet low enough for chef to be part of conversations. Door on left will lead to projected screened porch. (Photos by Tom Hopkins.)

THE HOPKINS BARN HOUSE

L-shaped deck on the south side of the Hopkins barn house is used as present entry to main living area on second floor. Stairs to deck (not visible in photograph) are on west side. (Top right) Linseed-oiled pine floors lead directly to bedroom ahead (soon to be a nursery). Glass-paneled swinging doors were retrieved by Tom's brother, a builder, from a nineteenth-century house he was renovating. (Bottom right) Bright U-shaped kitchen is well lighted during the day by roof skylights and sliding glass door at entryway. Swivel strip lighting takes over at night. Dining area is on right as you enter. (Photos by Tom Hopkins.)

THE TOWNSEND MOORE BARN

(Bottom left) Southeast view of stone-and-frame barn house. Barn-red siding is highlighted by 24-inch stone walls, painted white, which surround the building on three sides. Covered terrace was created after wood-framed south wall was taken down, a cool spot on hot summer days. (Top right) Dining room is suffused with light from large stationary window on left, highlighting beauty of exposed ceiling timbers and polished elegance of dining table and chairs. Antique pine corner cupboard and chest are nice foils for darker wood. Note old pewter chandelier over table and lovely flower arrangement (a Bubbles specialty). Kitchen door is straight ahead. (Bottom right) Stud-built kitchen addition, 12 feet by 30 feet, on west side, includes family dining space at north end. In keeping with other rooms, ceiling is treated with wooden rafters in similar fashion (except for fan, unique to the cook's domain). (Photos by Tom Hopkins.)

THE COWLES BARN HOUSE

(Top) Barn house and other buildings with all lights on. A spectacular sight in the middle of the flat Minnesota cornfields. (Photo by Gene Lindman.) (Bottom) Dining and living areas as seen from kitchen. Upholstered seating in far corner is built-in, as are bookcases. Vermont Castings wood stove on raised hearth is gathering place for all. Freestanding chimney wall is seen behind stove. Designed by owner, this monumental work is faced with hundreds of hand-crafted, glazed tiles. Flooring is Vermont slate and, in sitting area, oak. (Photo by Janet A. Null, A.I.A.)

Think Creatively

Because of its very nature, a barn house offers opportunities for many creative ideas. John O'Brien, for example, added a silo to his barn house to accommodate spiral stairs that, if set inside the house, would have taken up floor space he preferred to leave open. The Townsend Moores removed the entire south wall of their barn to create a sheltered terrace on the ground floor and a large covered porch off the second-floor master bedroom. Several barn houses in this book show ways to capture solar heat—sun rooms, greenhouses, or, as with the Cowles', a south wall set at an optimum angle for solar gain.

Skylights work well in barn houses, for they provide light to large as well as small areas, along with ventilation, and they also eliminate the need for additional windows that can detract from the barnlike look of the house. Lofts, too, are versatile, serving as extra bedrooms, a study, a library, or something entirely unique to your barn house. In addition, they provide an overview of the room below. Balconies, large stair landings, and in-between levels, such as Jill Butler's, are other attractive ways of gaining views of space with open ceilings.

Draw Your Own Plans

This is the route taken by many barn house owners in this book. If your home-drawn plans don't meet the requirements of the local building department of your lender, have an architect, designer, or draftsperson redraw them. Actually, it's smart to have a professional look over your plans anyway. He or she may have some good suggestions. And if you are going to build a post-and-beam house, have an experienced timber framer determine the sizes and spacing of the timbers.

A good friend to help in planning is Ramsey and Sleeper's *Architectural Graphic Standards*. This is the "bible" for architects, designers, and builders, for it is loaded with essential data needed in planning. The book—

it's a big one—illustrates the correct way to indicate various materials—brick, stone, stud walls, and so on. It gives dimensions for standard pieces of furniture—beds, dining tables, sofas, various kinds of chairs, coffee tables—and even shows how much space should be allowed around each piece. It gives layouts for kitchens and baths, illustrates the space required for a flight of standard stairs and for spiral stairs, and even tells you how much shelf space is required for each type of glass stemware. You'll also find standard dimensions for windows and doors, details on fireplaces and mantels, and lots of other data to help you plan.

Graphic Standards is expensive, around $135 a copy. If you don't care to spend this sort of money (and unless you are a pro, you probably won't), check your library or ask if it can get a copy on loan from another public library. The earlier editions have more data on residential requirements. The newer are more geared to the commercial market.

A good way to start planning is to draw the approximate dimensions of each floor or level on tracing paper. Then draw circles to indicate major rooms and areas. This procedure will show you how each room relates to the other. You may use several sheets of tracing paper and draw a good many circles before you get a basic layout that seems to work. See if it still works when you draw it to scale on ¼-inch graph paper. Allow each square to represent one foot, and don't be concerned about inches at this stage of the game. Give dimensions of each room and major area, then add windows, doors, closets, bathroom fixtures, etc.

Study the plan to see what works or what might be wrong. Does the front entry, for example, open directly into the living room? Wouldn't you prefer an entry hall with a closet before going into the living room? Do you have to go through one bedroom to reach a bathroom that serves two bedrooms? Do some rooms have too many doors? Have you put the plumbing in one central core to simplify installation? Are the rooms large enough to accommodate your furniture? If you have a king-size or queen-size bed, a large dining table that seats ten, an enormous sofa—these are all things to think about. Also—if you like a large country kitchen—is there room for a fireplace or wood stove?

Rework the plan until you are reasonably certain that it represents what you want in a house. Put the plan aside for a day or two so you can "sleep on it." If it still looks good, it probably is. Now all you have to do is to find someone to build your barn house, or go about building it yourself.

CHAPTER NINE

Find the Right Contractor or Restorationist

You can avoid spending a lot of money for unnecessary work and forgo a lot of headaches if you get the right person to handle the conversion of your antique barn into a comfortable home. If you are building a new barn-style house, you also need workmen who have respect for the way barns are put together.

The woods are full of builders and general contractors who can do a good job of building or remodeling a conventional house, but not all of them know braced-frame, heavy timber construction. And there is a world of difference between stick-built or stud construction and timber frame methods. Not only is the actual framing different, but different skills are required. The way in which all other components of the barn house are installed—plumbing, heating, wiring, insulation—also differs from conventional house construction.

For a first-rate job you need someone who has had experience restoring old houses and, especially, with converting barns into houses. This is especially important if you plan to dismantle and reassemble an old barn. For this ticklish and demanding job you will need a real expert, someone who knows traditional joinery methods and has had experience applying them.

It is not essential that such a person be a general contractor. He, or occasionally she, can be a master carpenter, a restorationist, or a master builder. Such an individual can oversee your entire project and coordinate the other trades involved—plumbing, electrical, masonry, and so on. He will probably recommend people he has worked with on other jobs and whose work he likes.

It is also important that the person you select be not only a "barn nut" but also someone you'll be able to talk to and feel comfortable with. Some craftspeople can be difficult to deal with—they are prima donnas and want to be left alone to do it their way and no other. We know of at least one master carpenter who can even intimidate the architect—no small accomplishment. You want someone who will respect your opinions—after all, it *is* your house—and who will, if he differs with you, explain why he thinks it important to do things another way.

Once you've found the right person, or think you have, ask for the names of people he or she has worked for. Talk with some of them before you make any definite commitment. Ask if they are pleased with the work, if there were unexpected snags that might have been prevented, or if there were large cost overruns. If possible, go around and see the finished job.

Here are a few sources that may help you in your search for just the right person:

Local and Regional Newspapers

Among your best bets are local publications. They are useful in many ways, not least to get a feeling of the general atmosphere of the area. The classified ads are where you are likely to get names of builders, contractors, timber framers, restorationists, barn builders, and tradespeople.

In addition, call a large regional paper and ask for the editorial department or the editor of the home, living, or real estate section. See if they have done any recent features on barn conversions—these make good stories and are very popular with readers—or on barn-style houses. Try to get copies of any stories they might have done. You'll learn a lot, including the names of the owners and probably of the builder, contractor, or renovator as well.

Local Historical Societies

They may be able to refer you to people who have done restorations on antique timber frame dwellings and barns. They may be able to give you the names of homeowners, whom you can then ask for the names of the people who did the work for them.

Architects

A local architect who specializes in restorations can probably give you the names of builders, contractors, and tradespeople he has worked with and found satisfactory.

Local Building Officials

While the building inspector probably won't want to recommend one carpenter or builder over another, he can no doubt give you the names of local people who have done work on barn conversions or new barn houses.

Members of the Timber
Framers Guild

If there is a guild member nearby, he may be able to suggest someone to handle your project or may perhaps handle the job himself. You can write for a referral to the Timber Framers Guild of North America, P.O. Box 1046, Keene, New Hampshire 03431.

Lucking Out

Keep your eyes peeled for barn renovations or new barn-style houses as you make your rounds across your chosen territory. If you see something under construction that looks like a barn, stop for a minute and chat with the workmen on the job. Try to find out the name of the owner and the contractor or builder. If the barn is finished or being lived in, you could knock at the door, or check with the tax assessor at Town Hall for the owner's name. Most owners, if asked, will give a frank opinion about a contractor or builder who did work for them. If he was good, they'll be happy to tell you. If not—they'll tell you that, too.

Many states require builders and remodelers to have a license but this is not necessarily an indication of the quality of the work. Even the fact that the contractor or builder is a member of a building trade association is no guarantee that he or she does quality work. Word of mouth still is the best way to line up good people.

CHAPTER TEN

How Much Work Can You Do Yourself?

You can do a lot. If there are two of you, you can do a lot more—and it's nice to have company. Many of the barn houses we showcase in this book are shining examples of what two—or sometimes more—dedicated people can accomplish when they really put their minds (and hearts) to it and dig in.

Sometimes that digging in can be for a long haul, but every DIY veteran we've talked to says that, in the end, it was worth it—sweat, tears, calloused hands, and all. Given the cost of labor today, the money you save can amount to a sizable sum. And so can your positive feelings of accomplishment and pride—not to mention the end result: your finished barn house.

Deb and Mark Mohler, for example, when converting their limestone barn in Clay County, Kansas, figure they saved $15,000 or more by taking on some of the jobs that would ordinarily be contracted to others. They began by clearing out the accumulated junk of decades from the barn itself, then, with pick and shovel, dug out countless inches of hardened manure that covered the first floor. Later, they paneled walls and ceilings with salvaged planks and did other finish work (see page 87 for more about the Mohler renovations). Another couple, Nancy and Gary Miers, did so much work on their barn house in Maine that they figure they saved at least $40,000. (Their story is also detailed in this book.)

Aside from dedication to the job at hand, how much work you can actually do yourself depends on several things. First, your physical strength and stamina. Then, how quickly you can acquire new skills. Next, the amount of time you can devote to the project and how much help you can count on from friends and relatives. And finally, local building codes that might prohibit you from doing certain jobs yourself, like wiring or plumbing.

Building Codes

These exist almost everywhere, except possibly in some rural areas. There are state codes and often local codes as well, all enforced by the building inspector. Some codes are very strict and require that all plumbing, wiring, and heating be done only by a licensed mechanic. Other codes are less restrictive, if your work can pass the building inspector, you're okay. Most people prefer to leave jobs like plumbing, central heating, and especially wiring to professionals anyway. Insurance companies prefer this, too. So, unless you are an experienced electrician or plumber, or have taken courses in these trades, you're probably better off—and safer—to do the same, even if your local codes would allow you to do the work yourself.

How Much Time You Can Spend

The amount of time you can devote to the project is, of course, of prime importance. Working on weekends and during vacations will get you there eventually, but if you can manage to also work evenings and weekdays you're going to speed things up considerably. If you didn't make the teaching profession your career choice, this will certainly be the time you'll wish you had. The whole summer off—oh, boy!

Stamina

You'll need a good measure of stamina—harder to muster in late afternoons or evenings after eight hours or so at your regular job. Even relatively nontaxing work like painting, which is easy enough when you're fresh and rested, is quite another matter when you're tired to begin with.

Perseverance

Plain, old-fashioned stick-to-itive-ness is going to be one of your most valuable assets. If you are doing much of the work yourselves, the job at times can seem almost endless. Indeed, we know of at least two couples who gave up and sold out—they simply couldn't take it anymore; and many couples warn, "If your marriage is shaky—look out." Discouraging as this may sound, it's better to be realistic about what's ahead than to plunge in all starry-eyed and end up bogged down in disappointment and frustration. The job can be done—be assured of that—and the people in this book are living proof.

Physical Strength

Muscle aplenty is called for, too. A 4-by-8-foot sheet of gypsum wallboard weighs in at about 60 pounds. A bundle of asphalt shingles runs around 70 pounds. If you're handling big timbers such as the posts and beams needed for framing, you'll need several pairs of strong arms—hopefully from helpful friends and neighbors. And it takes more than two strong backs to handle a 14-foot-long, 8-by-8-foot oak post that can weigh around 400 pounds. What you need most to handle this are not only strong arms but a crane.

If you are building from scratch, when it comes time to frame the roof, the crane and several helpers with experience and know-how will be a welcome addition. At barn-raising time, the whole neighborhood, plus all the extended family you can corral, will be needed. After that, there's a celebration and lots of good stuff to eat. Then they all go home and you and yours begin the finish work.

Acquiring New Skills

The ability to acquire new skills is extremely important. Many more techniques are needed besides knowing how to drive a nail or saw a straight-line cut. Roofing, insulating, drywalling, flooring, tiling, and so on all require specialized skills. If you're planning to do your own plumbing and wiring, you would be wise to find a technical school that gives courses in the basics. Home centers sell videotapes and books on these and related subjects and can be extremely helpful with technical advice on all kinds of building questions. One in particular, Home Depot, an expanding chain of building supply supermarkets in many states, makes a point of hiring former building professionals who can teach customers how to do all kinds of tasks related to home building. They even make free house calls.

Supercenters such as these can be helpful in other ways, too, because once you establish credit with them, you can get the majority of your necessary materials there and not have the bother of dealing with several different suppliers and setting up separate credit lines. It is a good idea to establish credit at a local lumberyard, too. You can get all or most of your lumber needs filled there, in addition to bricks, cement blocks, and so on. (Find a lumberyard that doesn't charge for delivery each time you order something.) Whether you are dealing with a lumberyard, a plumbing supply house, or one of the home centers, be sure to ask for the contractor's discount. This could be as much as 10 percent and maybe an additional 5 percent if you pay promptly.

In addition to home centers, many bookstores have special sections devoted to building techniques for the tyro, and so does your local library (see bibliography). There are also more and more videotapes becoming available that show "how to" in great detail. Many manufacturers of specific building products offer detailed specification and instructional literature and also audio- and videotapes. You can get these at home centers, which tend to cater more to DIYers than do building supply centers, which are geared to professionals. It certainly pays to have a look at all of these offerings, but nothing can match hands-on experience. For this your best bet is one of the schools that teaches potential do-it-yourselfers the basics they should know before embarking on either a renovation or a new building.

The Shelter Institute in Bath, Maine, is one of the better-known schools of this type. It was started in 1974 by Patsy and Pat Henin and has taught thousands of hopefuls of all ages, from all over this country and many foreign countries, how to build their own homes. Courses run one, two, and three weeks, and weekend courses are also given. The one-week course in post-and-beam construction is ideal for would-be barn house owners. Student builders participate in the actual construction of a 20-by-30-foot post-and-beam frame and learn basic mortise-and-tenon joinery techniques, layout, and design. The Henins are generous with meticulous sharing of their know-how about all phases of home building, including laying foundations and site concepts. In addition to the course in post-and-beam construction, Shelter Institute has courses in other types of house framing. When you register, you are sent a list of accommodations available in the area, including campgrounds, bed-and-breakfast places, motels, and so on. Shelter Institute has a mail-order business with a wide selection of books and videotapes for sale or rent. Another offering is a complete precut post-and-beam frame in a kit for those who are ready to build. This is the kit that Nancy and Gary Miers used to build their barn house.

In Berkeley, California, the Owner-Builder Center offers similar courses, including its Summer Building Camp in Grass Valley, where hands-on house building is taught. They also have ongoing seminars in various areas of the state on a wide range of building topics. One subject that can be of particular value is the owner/contractor course, which shows you how to supervise your own building project and how to deal with subcontractors (see sources).

The General Contractor Is You

Serving as your own general contractor is an excellent way to save money (from 10 to 25 percent of total construction costs) and control overall spending. If you are a well-organized person but don't feel you have the time, talent, or inclination to get deeply involved in do-it-yourself projects for your barn house, you should give this option serious consideration. Getting bids on the work to be done is the first step. This means interviewing the various subcontractors—plumbing, heating, masonry, electrical, carpentry, and so on. You should have a floor plan or design sketch to show them and a list of specifications for the materials you want to use. For this, you would be well advised to first consult an architect or house designer. Most will consult on an hourly basis and will advise you on quality materials—and on ways you might save money without sacrificing quality.

It's a good idea to get bids from at least two or more subcontractors in each trade. You will then make the decision on the basis not only of price but on the contractor's reputation, jobs he has completed (ask to see some), and—important, since you'll be seeing a good deal of each other—a feeling that you can work well together.

When the contract is drawn up, make sure it includes both a start and a completion date, and a clause stating that specified amounts are to be paid as each portion of the work is finished. The contractor must have liability insurance, so that any injuries on the job will be covered. (You, too, should have liability insurance.) Make sure the contract says that you will receive a lien waiver, stating that all workers and suppliers have been paid, and that the contractor is responsible for having work checked by the building inspector as required and will leave the building site clean, removing all debris and discarded materials.

When acting as your own general contractor, you are responsible for scheduling all work so that one job follows another in the correct sequence. This means, for example, that you have to keep a close eye on the progress of the plumber so that as his work nears completion you can make sure that the drywall people are lined up and ready to come in. You want to make sure that the carpenters don't stand around idly or go off to another job while waiting for the electrician, the roofer, or whichever job must be done before they can start again. You also want to be available to make decisions when required. And once you make a decision, try to stick with it. Changing your mind can be expensive—you pay to have the work done, then pay to have it undone, and then pay again to have it done the way you have now decided it should have been done. Besides, if you are constantly changing your mind, the subcontractors will soon figure that you don't know what you want and will lose respect for you.

You also want to double-check on whether the work has been inspected by the local building inspector and at the proper time. If an inspection on the job is skipped or overlooked, the inspector could insist that the completed work be taken apart and opened for inspection before the work gets the okay. This can cost you both time and money.

The real art of being a good general contractor lies in being well organized, scheduling correctly, making sure that all necessary supplies and materials are on hand, and being available when decisions must be made, while still not being so ubiquitous that you get in the crews' hair and slow things down. Always be certain that your home and business phone numbers are posted in a prominent place so you can be reached quickly if necessary.

When you're on the job site in person, save the jokes and anecdotes until quitting time. This is also a good time to check with the crew leader or foreman about supplies needed for the next day's—or next week's— needs, so you can order ahead. If you are on the job site and something is needed right away, save an hour or more in pay by being the "gofer" yourself rather than having one of the workmen do it.

You're the boss, so the question "Who's in charge around here?" should never have to be raised. That's being a successful general contractor.

Proper Dress for the Occasion

If you are going to do a lot of the hard and dirty work yourself, wear the right clothes. This means work shoes with thick, nonskid soles and sides high enough to protect the ankles; long pants, not too tight; a long-sleeved shirt; and leather work gloves. For some jobs, like wire brushing old beams, installing fiberglass insulation, or sanding joints between dry-wall panels, you'll need a face mask and safety goggles to keep accumulated dirt, dust, and minute fibers out of your eyes and lungs. To protect your head from falling debris, a hard hat is a good idea.

Keep Healthy and Be Safe

Before you start any barn renovation, be sure your tetanus protection is up-to-date (doctors say a booster every ten years is necessary). If you've never had a tetanus series, now's the time to start one. It is important to be protected against tetanus when working around barns, especially around stalls and stables where livestock was kept. And we've all been warned about stepping on a rusty nail. You need tetanus protection on new construction, too, for you can get a deep, nasty cut if you are not careful.

In hot weather drink plenty of water or soft drinks—not beer. Eat lightly and give yourself time to digest your food before taking on any really heavy work. If you're not used to hard physical work, take frequent short breaks. You'll toughen up soon enough.

When you're tired near the end of a hard day's work, don't take on unfamiliar or complicated tasks. Leave these jobs until the next day, when you're rested and fresh. The best thing to do when you've about had it for the day is to sweep up and quit. A clear area in the morning makes for a better start.

Make sure you have all the right tools and materials to get you through a particular project. It's a nuisance and a big waste of time to have to stop work and drive to the nearest hardware store or lumberyard if you've run out of something vital. (And it's always Sunday or a long holiday weekend when this happens.) Make a detailed shopping list ahead of time.

Good-quality tools are a must, as is a good tool chest. If you make a point of returning a tool to the chest as soon as you've finished with it, you'll save a lot of hunting around for a misplaced hammer or chisel or whatever it was you were just using yesterday, or perhaps just an hour ago. And never, never, leave a tool on top of a stepladder. Aside from the fact that the tool will be hard to find, it will also be a real hazard. Move the ladder, and the hammer, pry bar, or whatever, may be on its way down. Save your head—you'll need it. And a word of caution about ladders: always be sure that they are set at the correct angle and rest on a solid, even base. Keep both wood and metal ladders clear of electric wires, for both can conduct electricity. Call your utility company if any wires must be removed.

Finally, keep a little medical kit on hand. A liquid antiseptic such as peroxide or Betadine for minor cuts and scratches and assorted sizes of Band-Aids are a must. For more serious injuries, get thee to a doctor.

CHAPTER ELEVEN

Building Your Own Barn House

If you're your own builder, you can knock as much as 50 percent off the cost of your barn house. This is the route many young people—and some not so young—are taking today. They just can't afford the going rate for a decent home.

It takes a lot of time, energy, and dedication to build your own home, but those who have done it say the satisfaction and pride, not to mention the money saved, is well worth the effort.

Be forewarned, though, that not all banks look with favor on the owner/builder. You are more apt to get mortgage money if you build with a kit (see sources).

Most owner building occurs in small towns and rural areas where land prices are apt to be lower and where there are fewer restrictive building codes. Labor, too, is apt to be lower in these areas, a plus if you'll need some outside help. And in rural areas you are more likely to find lumberyards or sawmills that can provide you with the large timbers you'll need.

Do Your Homework

Learn as much as you can about house construction before you begin. Read books, look at videotapes, take owner/builder courses. Reliable information on how to find these things is given in sources and chapter 10. You'll find salespeople at home centers and local lumberyards helpful. And if you are building with a post-and-beam kit, the outfit you bought it from will answer questions regarding the erection of the frame and other related subjects. Some, as part of the deal, will send experienced workers to put up the frame.

Work from Plans

Experienced owner/builders advise you to work from detailed plans, either stock plans modified to suit your needs or your own plans drawn with the help of experienced house designers or architects. In any event, don't wing it. Detailed plans are essential for the amateur builder. The experienced carpenter/builder may not need such plans to see how things should be put together, but you do. Also, don't start out with too grandiose a plan—keep the core house small. You can always expand later on. And unless you are buying a post-and-beam kit, get an architect or timber framer to design your basic frame and to specify sizes and spacing of timbers.

Before You Begin to Build

Try to start construction in the spring. This will give you many weeks of mild weather with long working days. You'll need a lot of daylight hours to get the house framed and made weathertight before rainy or cold weather sets in. After the structure is enclosed, electricity can be brought in so that you can do the inside work during the winter months.

You'll probably need a building permit before you can start work. When you go to the local building department for your permit, ask to meet the building inspector. It's good to know him, and for him to know you. A friendly inspector can give you a lot of good tips, since many are retired builders or general contractors. Also, if you are on good terms, he will probably make a special effort to get over promptly when it's time to make an inspection.

On some jobs you are going to need helpers. Try to line them up before you will be needing them. Friends and relatives will, of course, generally work for free—or at least for less than the going rate. But they may not have much experience in building and may not be able always to show up when you need them. So unless you have experienced and reliable free labor, assume you'll probably have to hire professionals for special jobs. Again, contract these pros and line them up before you need them.

Also be sure to have liability insurance to protect yourself if anyone gets hurt working on your property. Friends and relatives can sue, too.

First Things First

Have your percolation tests made, your septic system installed, and your well drilled as soon as you have selected the building site. These essential and expensive installations should be gotten quickly out of the way, since their location may determine the exact building site. You can't, for example, have a house or a well too close to a septic system. Codes specify the minimum distance they must be set apart from each other.

It is a good idea to build a little shack near the building site. Use the shack to store your tools and small materials. Also, if you can get electric power brought into the shack, you'll be able to use power tools and heat a can of beans on a hot plate. You might even install a telephone, so you can keep in touch with the outside world. If you can't bring electricity into the site yet, consider buying or renting a portable generator.

The Foundation

A foundation plan is usually supplied with a post-and-beam kit. If no plan is provided, or if you have designed your own place, have an architect or house designer draw the foundation plan.

Foundations must be accurate, true, and level. If the foundation has been properly installed, it makes all the rest of the work simpler. But if it is off, even by just an inch or two, it can cause a lot of future headaches. Errors in the foundation can affect framing and other areas of construction, and trying to compensate can mean a lot of wasted time and effort. Get the best mason you can find for this job.

When the foundation is poured, anchor bolts should be set in the concrete to secure the sills. Ask the mason to install the sills. These should be made of pressure-treated lumber that is decay-and-insect-proof and there should be a sealer between the sill and foundation wall to reduce air infiltration. The sill should be wide enough to accommodate insulation for the outside walls. Use a 2-by-12 sill if the insulation is to be applied between 2-by-4 studding set *outside* the posts. If the insulated wall is run *between* the posts, a 2-by-8 sill will be adequate. If a large timber sill is to be set on top of the lower sill anchored to the foundation, the two sills can be joined with metal straps.

The Floor

As soon as the sills are in place, install the girder(s), the floor beams (joists), and the subflooring, which can be boards or exterior-grade plywood. Now you'll have a solid work platform for the rest of the construction.

The Frame

Framing timbers are very heavy, so unless you have a good many strong helpers, you'll need a forklift or a crane to help unload them when they are delivered to the site. Later, you may need a crane to help erect the frame and lift the roof rafters in place. A crane with operator may run $300 or so a day, but it can be worth it.

If you have bought a post-and-beam kit, an experienced crew should be on hand to erect the frame. This labor is usually included in the price of the kit. But if you are working with your own plan, erecting the frame may be up to you. This is hard, demanding, and sometimes dangerous work, and, in addition to your regulars, you should have at least one or two helpers with experience in post-and-beam construction. You'll also need a come-along. This is a hand-operated winch used to pull joints together. You should be able to get one at a tool rental shop.

Make the House Weathertight

As soon as the frame is erected, install the roof sheathing and roofing. Also apply sheathing to the outside walls. Once these jobs are done you will have a dry place to store materials and be able to work on inside jobs on rainy days. You should also install windows and exterior doors as soon as you can.

Roughing-in

As soon as you have framed the interior partitions, arrange to have the basic heating, plumbing, and wiring installed. These are jobs you can do yourself if you know what you are doing and there are no local codes to prevent it. If you have a knack for this sort of work, you could read up on these subjects and get some videotapes. If you don't have that kind of talent, you'd better take a couple of courses or get in a heating contractor, a plumber, and an electrician. You want to get these basic installations—the roughing-in—done and checked by the building inspector before you move on to any finish work.

Finish Work

This is the long haul, where you separate the men from the boys, the women from the girls. Many who have built their own barn houses have told us that the finish work is the worst part of the entire project. It does seem to take forever.

What finish work actually involves is installing the drywall for walls and ceilings, taping the joints between sections, coating the tape with joint compound, waiting for it to dry and then sanding it smooth, then applying additional coats of compound, letting them dry, sanding again, and continuing this routine until the joints are completely concealed. Fun, what? Oh yes, be sure to wear a face mask when you sand, unless you use a wet sanding block.

Finish work also includes installing the interior doors and the wood trim around doors and windows. Then you spackle over nailheads and joints, sand some more, and then paint. And now there are walls and ceilings to paint.

Finish work also means installing kitchen cabinets, work counters and fixtures, and bathroom fixtures. And finally, when you think you are all done, there is the matter of floors. The subfloor has to be covered, with wood, vinyl sheeting, vinyl tile, ceramic tile, or slate. And then the baseboards or base moldings have to be installed.

Yes, it does seem to go on forever, but eventually it gets completed. After that—if you still have the same mate or companion you started with—you can begin to enjoy the barn house you built yourselves.

CHAPTER TWELVE

Solutions to Special Problems of the Barn House

Barn houses differ from conventionally built houses in that installation of certain key elements—heating systems, plumbing, wiring—can present special problems that must be handled in somewhat different fashion. Newer ways of insulating walls and roofs are being used, along with newer materials. These can be difficult to handle if workers are inexperienced or unfamiliar with the products and the techniques of installation. Insuring adequate ventilation is important, too. This can be a problem in a barn house. Here are some workable solutions and a few tips on adding space, finishes for timbers, and getting up to a barn house loft.

No matter how you go about building your barn house, whether you have a general contractor, work with an architect or designer, act as your own general contractor, or are building it yourself, the first thing you want to do is go over your building plans with your contractor and/or any subcontractors you've lined up—the electrician, the plumber, the heating engineer—so that they know what is being done and can make advance plans. They'll want to order supplies, line up workmen, and schedule their time.

If they have experience in working with barn houses, some of these people may have suggestions on how to modify the plans to simplify installation, save money, or get better results. Each of them will want to do his basic roughing-in while the framework is open and exposed, well before any finish work is started. Here's where you will want to do some scheduling of your own so that they don't all show up at the same time.

Heating

There are two types of central heating suitable for a barn house— forced warm air and circulating hot water (hydronic). Either system, properly designed and installed, will keep the house comfortable. Each has certain advantages and disadvantages. The choice, therefore, can be based on personal preference and/or cost. In addition, other heating systems may be considered in certain climates or for parts of the house.

Forced Warm Air In a forced warm air system the air is heated in a fuel-fired (oil, gas, coal, or wood) furnace. The furnace blower forces the heated air through large pipes—ducts—to outlet registers in the floors or walls. There will also be several "cold air returns"—registers and ducts to carry the cooled air back to the furnace to be reheated. If the system is properly designed, there should be a gentle flow of warm air coming out of the registers, not a strong blast of hot air. The same ducts and registers used to heat the house in winter may also be used to cool it in summer by the addition of a central air conditioner, either alongside or combined with the furnace.

In a barn house with open planning there may not be interior partitions of sufficient depth to accommodate the large ducts that are required. One practical, and very attractive, solution to this problem is to leave the ducts exposed and paint them. In the Bloom-Gwillim barn house, the ducts become a decorative element as they soar straight up from the living room level to the second floor. Painted a deep slate blue, these 20-odd-inch columnar ducts have a very contemporary, high-tech look that is both sculptural and dramatic (see page 81).

Achieving comfortable and even heat in a large two-story-high area can be a problem with forced warm air because the heat inevitably rises to the ceiling, leaving the lower level of the room on the cool side. One way to deal with this is to have a cold air return installed near the peak or at a high point in the ceiling. This will move the accumulated air back into the system. A more common solution, used in many barn houses, is to install one or two large ceiling fans with blades slanted to force the heated air downward.

Circulating Hot Water   In a top-quality circulating-hot-water heating system, water is heated in a boiler and carried by small-diameter pipes to baseboard units, or wall panels. These are specially designed to project *radiant heat*. Radiant heat is like the sun—it warms objects in its path rather than the air around objects. *Convected heat* warms the air.

We can thank the Europeans for many of the improvements made in the design of circulating-hot-water systems—a form of heating commonly used in Europe, where energy costs are far higher than ours. As a consequence, Europeans have expended considerable time and effort on designing systems that can squeeze the most heat out of every gallon of oil or cubic foot of gas.

Circulating-hot-water heat can also be used in floors, with coils embedded underneath flooring transforming an entire area into one big, radiant heat panel. This is a good system to use in a two-story room. Floor temperatures can be kept at a comfortable 70 to 80 degrees without allowing an excessive amount of heat to concentrate at the top of the ceiling or under the roof.

The main drawback to a radiant-heated floor is cost. The floor must be framed to carry a considerable load: several inches of lightweight concrete, many feet of tubing filled with water, and the finish floor—usually clay tile, slate, or stone. It's handsome, efficient, and expensive.

Electric Heat   This option is worth considering if a house is very well insulated and there are favorable electric rates.

One type of electric heat is produced by the *heat pump*. This unit will heat the house on the same principle as the refrigerator or the room air conditioner. It is designed so that, in cold weather, heat is extracted from outside air and distributed throughout the house through ducts and registers. In hot weather, it extracts the heat from inside the house and pumps it outdoors. There is a resistance heater in the unit that will go on automatically and provide heat when the outdoor temperature is so low that the pump cannot extract sufficient heat from the outside air.

Heat pumps have been popular in milder climates for many years, and advances in design have now made them suitable for colder regions as well. Before installing one, however, be sure to find out the cost-to-operate in your area and the cost-to-operate in a barn house with its extra-high ceilings.

Electric heat has been used for some time in baseboard units, but in a large space it is not very efficient. It's convenient, however, in bathrooms and other small areas. In rooms with average 7-foot or 8-foot ceilings, a type of radiant heat using coils set into drywall works well and is easily installed. One nice thing about this is that it eliminates the need for registers or baseboard units, thus freeing floor space.

Whether you end up using either baseboard units or ceiling panels, you can install separate thermostats in each room to help reduce electric bills.

Wood Stoves A well-designed wood stove of the proper size can easily provide all the heat required for a well-insulated, moderate-sized, open-plan barn house. The open plan insures that the heat will flow to all areas of the house. This can be an inexpensive way to heat where wood is readily available at a reasonable price.

But, because wood stoves and wood furnaces require daily attention, people who do heat with wood usually also have a standby automatic heating system that will take over should the wood fire go out, or if the owners want to get away for a night or two or for a vacation. Several barn houses in this book are heated with wood. All have standby heating systems.

Fireplaces Even a Rumsford-design fireplace or one equipped with glass-panel screens is not as efficient as a good wood stove. And the ordinary fireplace can waste even more heat than it provides. On the other hand, a fireplace is handy for taking the chill off on days when central heat is not required. And there are few things as pleasant as sitting by an open fire on a cold winter evening. At our house, and in many houses, this pleasure is well worth the few extra dollars gone up the chimney.

Passive Solar Heat Free heat from the sun will reduce the cost of operating any type of heating system.

You can introduce so-called passive solar heat into your house with large, south-facing glass areas and strategically placed skylights on the south side of the roof. Clerestory windows on this side are an additional way to capture heat from the sun. In cool climates, a type of glass called "Low-E" (low-emissivity) can be installed to reduce heat loss. This special glazing allows the sun's rays to enter, then reflects radiant heat back into the room. This glass is said to be 50 or more percent effective in reducing energy costs than ordinary double glazing. It also cuts down on condensation and glare. If ordinary double glazing is used for windows and skylights, all glass areas should be covered with thermal curtains or shades to reduce heat loss at night.

Many of these windows and other glass areas will, of course, be doing double duty by also providing natural light, ventilation, and views, so they are especially cost effective. Doing double duty also can be slate, brick, or clay-tile floors set on a thick concrete slab directly in the path of the incoming sun. Such floors act as thermal storage units, absorbing heat during the day and releasing it to the house at night. A masonry fireplace and chimney, placed correctly, serves as an excellent thermal unit. It should be carefully planned.

If you live in the Southwest or another region where there is intense winter sunlight, you will need a far smaller expanse of glass in order to achieve solar gain. In fact, too much glass will cause the house to become overheated. Tinted glass, a type that reflects heat back to the sun is desirable in areas of the house where you don't require solar gain.

There are even more specialized ways to achieve passive solar heat, but these should be carefully assessed to make sure that the heat gained justifies the additional cost of design and installation and also whether they would be aesthetically pleasing in your barn house. One of these is a masonry thermal storage wall made of brick, concrete, or stone. It is painted black or dark blue and set so as to catch the sun's rays. Black is a prime absorber of heat, so such a wall can retain a considerable amount for several hours after sunset.

Another specialized passive solar element is the "Trombe Wall," named after its originator, Felix Trombe. This is a thick masonry wall set on the south-facing exterior of a house. The outside face of the wall is completely covered with double glazing with an air space between the glass and masonry. This air space gets very warm, reaching 140 degrees F. during a sunny day. To tap into this heat, openings—called thermo-circulation vents—are located at the top and bottom of the wall. These allow natural air flow into the house, with the heated air rising to the top of the air space while the cool air from the house is drawn out through the bottom openings. These vents should always be equipped with dampers to keep reverse circulation from taking place at night.

A solar greenhouse can be an attractive and effective addition to your heating needs if properly designed and oriented. It is important that the wall between the greenhouse and main house be insulated, so that the house will not absorb excessive heat in summer or lose it on cold nights. In order to allow heat to flow into the house during the day and be kept in at night, an insulated glass door—single or double—should be installed in this wall. It can be opened during the day but at night the door and other openings in the wall should be closed. A vent leading from greenhouse to the outdoors is also necessary so that the space will not overheat in hot weather.

Solar Hot Water Heaters These fall into the so-called active solar heat category because they require roof collectors, pipes, pumps, and a storage tank. They can be highly cost effective, however, and pay for themselves in a relatively few years while providing your household with ample hot water. Your state's Department of Energy and your local utility company can give you information on this type of hot water heating. The yellow pages, too, list companies that specialize in this type of installation; look under "Solar Energy."

Whichever solar option you choose should be incorporated into the overall plan of your barn house early in the game. Your architect or house designer will be able to supply you with valuable information. Make sure to have a qualified firm do the installation. Also try to talk with people in the vicinity who have solar installations that were done by the firm you are considering.

Plumbing

Installing plumbing in a barn house is a bit more complicated than in a conventional house because interior walls will probably not be thick enough to carry the large-diameter waste lines to upstairs bathrooms. And these pipes, along with fresh-water pipes, should never be installed in outside walls where freezing can occur.

In order to simplify the installation, your plumber may suggest you rework your floor plan so that the upstairs baths are all located in the same core area. This may mean that only one set of waste lines has to be run to the second floor.

If there are no partitions in which the pipes can be run, the floor plan could perhaps be modified to include a downstairs closet that would accommodate the waste lines. The waste lines can also be enclosed in a hollow "beam" of wood made to look like the vertical posts. It is essential that this post be well insulated inside or else the sound of water rushing down the drain line will be all too apparent.

The plumber may also suggest that the ceiling underneath the upstairs bathroom be lowered a few inches in order to provide sufficient pitch for the horizontal drain lines. It is usually no big deal to "drop the ceiling" while the framing work is under way. But it can be an expensive and time-consuming chore if it has to be done after the ceiling has been covered with drywall. This is a good example of how important it is to find out beforehand what structural changes have to be made before work on heating, plumbing, and wiring is too far advanced.

Don't wait until the last minute to select bathroom fixtures and fittings. There is a wide range of these items to choose from and it can take a long time to make a final decision. If you don't decide what you want, you'll get what your plumber decides you want—or what he likes. By the way, colored fixtures cost a good deal more than white fixtures. And the cost of super-deluxe fittings—faucets, handles, and so on—can run more than the fixture itself.

Wiring

One of the first things your electrician will ask is what capacity electric service system you want—100 amps, 150 amps, 200 amps, or 400 amps. Unless you have a special need for unusual amounts of electric power, a 200-amp service entrance should be adequate.

Be sure to point out to your electrician that you don't want him to drill visible holes in your posts or beams. If he needs to get wires around them, have him drill holes where they won't be seen. Nor do you want him to chisel out a section of a post to accommodate a box for a wall switch. If a switch is required, have him set it on an adjacent wall.

There should be no difficulty running wiring in outside walls or interior partitions if they are framed with 2-by-3 or larger studding. The wall cavity will provide plenty of space for wiring and for outlet boxes. On outside walls, wiring is best done before the vapor barrier is applied, so that the barrier will not be torn as the electric work is done.

When there is no exterior wall cavity, as with stress-skin panels, other methods of wiring must be used. One way to accommodate the wiring is to cut grooves in the exterior wall material. The baseboard may also be set away from the wall with 1-by-2 or 2-by-2 wood strips so that the wiring can be run in back of the baseboard to outlet boxes also installed there.

When it is impractical to conceal the wires within the walls, the wiring can be surface-mounted. This is the way much of the wiring in Jill Butler's barn house was done (see page 117). Rigid metal conduits containing the wires and the outlet boxes were surface-mounted and look very appropriate in the casual barn atmosphere. If you want a high-tech look, the conduits can be painted a bright primary color—red, blue, green, or yellow. Surface-mounted wiring can also be handled with metal raceways.

While the electrician is doing the basic wiring, be sure that he provides outlets for any ceiling fans, for track lighting, or for any ceiling fixtures that will be hung from beams.

Insulation

There are several ways to insulate the walls of a post-and-beam house.

Insulate Between Studding   One approach is to run 2-by-4 studding between the framing and apply fiberglass insulation between the studs, which can be set 16 or 24 inches apart. The drawback here is that when the interior finish material—either drywall or wood paneling—is added, you lose about 4 inches of the timbers that would ordinarily be fully exposed.

If the studding is set on the outside face of the posts it will leave the interior framing exposed to its full depth—minus only the thickness of the drywall or paneling. This method allows the use of 2-by-6 studding, which can accommodate thicker insulation than the 2-by-4s. Insulation value of stud walls will be increased if rigid plastic foam panels are added.

The interior face, or room side, of the insulated stud wall should be covered with a *vapor barrier*. This plastic sheeting will help prevent moisture generated in the house from reaching the insulation and condensing. This would not only reduce efficiency of the insulation, but could cause paint on the exterior siding to blister and peel. It is also wise to cover the outside of the wall with an *air-infiltration barrier*. This barrier reduces movement of air inside the wall, thus improving the efficiency of the insulation.

One drawback to the stud wall method is that the drywall panels have to be cut to fit between the framing, leaving a seam where the drywall butts the timbers. Such seams can be covered with narrow wood molding or filled with caulking or spackle, but this can be a time-consuming chore.

Use Stress-skin Panels   The exterior frame of a post-and-beam structure can be sheathed with interlocking stress-skin panels—a laminated "sandwich" that provides exterior sheathing, insulation, and interior wall surface all in one package and produces an energy-efficient, rigid, airtight envelope. Since the panels are nailed to the outside of the frame and the interior face of the "sandwich" is prefinished with either drywall or wood paneling, there is no loss of depth of the exposed timbers as there is when studding is used and drywall is cut to fit between the framing.

Stress-skin panels are also available for roofs, if you want to leave the interior roof rafters exposed, as many timber frame owners do.

To be most effective, stress-skin panels must be properly installed. This can be tricky, and even some timber frame pros prefer to have a factory representative on hand to supervise installation of the panels. Some manufacturers suggest that installation time can be reduced and better results achieved if you send your plans to them so that correctly sized openings for windows and doors can be cut at the factory.

A 4-by-8-foot panel weighs around 120 pounds, so it's impractical to ship them any long distance. Today, however, manufacturers of these panels can be found all over the country. You can get the name of one

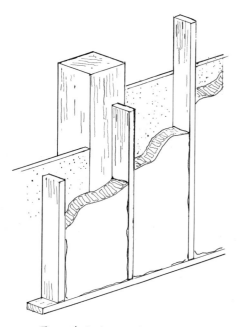

Insulated stud wall
set outside of posts

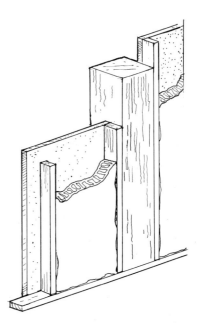

Insulated stud wall
set between posts

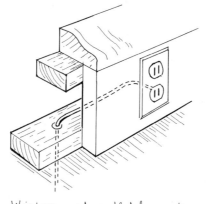

Wiring and outlet box set
behind furred-out baseboard

in your area by writing to the Structural Insulated Panel Association (see sources).

Some people have found that stress-skin panels make the house so airtight that they must install an air-to-air exchanger. This exhausts stale indoor air and replaces it with fresh outside air without any appreciable heat loss.

Other ways to insulate post-and-beam timber frame walls include those devised by John Bogaert in Connecticut and are described in the text on the Hogan house and used by Jonah Peterson in Indiana (see pages 129 and 151).

Insulate Stone Walls   The only way to insulate a stone wall and still leave the stone exposed on the outside is to build a stud wall that is set off from the interior wall. You then insulate between the studs as Jim Diserio did in his Pennsylvania barn house (see page 59).

If stone walls are not insulated they are apt to "sweat" in hot, humid weather and to be cold in winter. Even a 24-inch-thick wall does not have much insulating value, and while it will retain the heat it has absorbed in summer for a time, during the course of the winter it will become chilled.

Insulate the Roof   Because the roof of any house is a major source of both heat loss and gain, it needs even more insulation than the walls.

Stress-skin panels, as mentioned, are excellent for the roof. They also allow full-depth exposure of interior roof rafters, which is very attractive in a barn house. If you do not wish the rafters exposed, insulation can be applied between them, then covered with drywall.

The insulating capacity of the various brands and types of insulation is given as its "R-value." The higher the number—R16, R20, R30, and so on—the more insulation is provided. Your contractor, builder, or the local building inspector can tell you the R-value required for walls and roofs in your area.

Finishes for Timbers

Antique timbers don't need any protective finish. Restorationists and other lovers of antique timbers frown on anything that might destroy the warm patina of weathered wood, but do sometimes use a nontoxic oil for luster. New timbers don't have to have a finish either, but some timber framers and manufacturers of post-and-beam kits give the timbers a coating of penetrating oil or tung oil. This is done primarily so the timbers will not be stained or absorb dirt during shipping and erecting.

Some people may find a great deal of exposed wood a bit overpowering—especially if the wood is very dark. In this case, timbers can be given a coat of whitewash or a thin coat of white paint. This should be wiped down immediately so that only the grain of the wood absorbs the pigment. If you number any "old wood" purists among your friends, be prepared for horrified shock if you do decide to paint or whitewash any timbers. Jill Butler was going to give the antique timbers of her barn house a coat of whitewash but was talked out of it. Now she's glad. Remember, once the timbers have been coated with whitewash or paint, they can never be brought back to their original patina.

Ventilation

Skylights are a good way to get more natural ventilation into your barn house. Also, because they are set in the roof, skylights help maintain the "barny" look that too many windows will take away.

Super-skylights with remote controls are now available, and some even have moisture sensors that automatically close the skylight when a drop of rain hits the sensor.

Cupolas are another way to improve ventilation in a barn house and are very much in keeping with barn style. Old barns had cupolas to help remove the heat generated by hay and livestock. A cupola today can be equipped with a large fan to draw the warm air out of the house. In winter, all ventilating cupolas should have an insulated door or panel to prevent heat loss when closed.

In and Out of a Loft

Lofts are quite common in barn houses, and ladders are the cheapest and most space-conserving way to get up to a loft. For safety reasons, if you put in a ladder be sure it is secured at both top and bottom.

Ladders are fine for the young but they do lose their appeal as we age and become perhaps not as limber as we once were. When some friends of ours reached the time in their lives when the ladder to their sleeping loft lost its charm, they looked around for other ways to get there. They explored the possibility of a spiral staircase, which come in both metal and wood and look especially good in a barn house, but decided against one because their elderly parents visited frequently, and since one parent used a cane, they felt that problems might arise with a spiral staircase that could be avoided with stairs. They ended up building a small addition at the back of the kitchen/dining area, big enough to take a flight of stairs with a small space left over for a little utility room under the stairs. A decorative folding screen was used to cover the cleaning supplies and tools stashed away there.

Glossary

Acre. Unit of land measurement containing 43,560 square feet.

Active Solar Heat. Use of mechanical equipment such as roof collectors, pipes, pumps, and so on, to introduce solar heat into a building.

Adz. Axlike tool with a single blade at right angle to the handle. Used to shape logs into timbers.

Agreement for Sale. See *Contract for Sale.*

A.I.A. American Institute of Architects.

Air Infiltration Barrier. Sheet material applied over exterior wall sheathing to prevent cold outside air and rain from entering the wall cavity but that allows house-generated moisture to escape outdoors. Also called Building Wrap, House Wrap, Wind Barrier.

Air-to-air Heat Exchanger. Appliance that exhausts stale house air and brings in fresh outside air with minimum heat loss.

Anchor Bolts. Bolts set into the top of a foundation wall to secure wood sills.

Backfill. Replacement of excavated earth.

Backhoe. Earth-excavating machine with hoe on one end, shovel on other.

Balloon Frame. Form of stick-built construction with exterior wall studs running from sill to top plate.

Bank Barn. Barn set into a hill or slope so that its lower level opens onto grade.

Baseboard. Board that covers the joint between wall and floor.

Baseboard Heat. Heating element set in metal baseboard to provide heat from electricity or circulating hot water.

Batten. Narrow strip of wood covering a joint between boards. See *Board and Batten.*

Bay. Area between bents in a structure. Often used to describe the size of a barn, such as a "three-bay barn."

Beam. Horizontal load-bearing timber connected at each end to posts.

Bearing Wall. An interior wall or partition carrying some of the weight of the floor above. Cannot be removed unless provisions are made to support the floor.

Beetle. Heavy mallet used to drive wood pegs to secure wood joinery.

Berm. A narrow ledge or shelf of earth. Often used along a slope around barns to insure drainage and help insulate the lower portion of a stone wall.

Blueboard. Type of drywall suitable as a base for plaster or ceramic tile.

Board and Batten. Exterior wood siding consisting of vertically set wide boards with narrow battens applied over joints between boards.

Boiler. Unit where water is heated in a circulating-hot-water heating system.

Brace. A diagonally set timber that provides support.

Broadax. Ax with a broad single blade used to rough-shape logs into timbers.

BTU (British Thermal Unit). Standard measurement of heat. One BTU is the amount of heat needed to warm one pound of water to one degree Fahrenheit.

Building Codes. State and/or local regulations that specify construction of buildings.

Building Department. Local unit of government handling all aspects of building and renovation.

Building Inspector. Local official responsible for enforcement of building codes.

Building Lines. Lines fixed at a specified distance from road and adjoining property beyond which no structure can project.

Building Permit.   Issued by a local building department to allow work to be done on a building.

Building Wrap.   See *Air Infiltration Barrier.*

Bulldozer.   Earth-moving machine used to move dirt and rocks, rip out tree stumps, knock down buildings, etc.

CAD (Computer-Assisted Design).   Use of a computer to aid in drawing house plans, laying out wood joints, and other design tasks.

Cantilever.   That portion of a horizontal timber or structure extending beyond its vertical support.

Carpenter Ant.   Large black ant that builds nests by gnawing tunnels in sound timbers.

Casement Window.   A hinged window that opens and shuts like a door.

Caulking Compound.   A flexible, waterproof compound used for filling joints.

Chase (Chaseway).   A groove cut in wood, concrete, or other material to accommodate pipes, wiring, and other conduits.

Checking.   Fine cracks running lengthwise in a piece of lumber. Usually the result of shrinkage as wood is seasoned.

Chestnut.   Grayish-brown wood with pronounced grain. Until the American chestnut was destroyed by a blight in the early part of this century, this versatile wood was used for framing, sheathing, interior trim, floors, and roof shingles.

Chipboard.   Building panels made by compressing wood chips, sawdust, and a binding agent. Used for sheathing and subfloors.

Circulating-Hot-Water Heat.   Central heating system where water heated in a boiler is circulated by the aid of a small pump through pipes to radiators, baseboard units, wall panels, or coils set into the floor. Also called "hydronic heat."

Clapboard.   Horizontal exterior siding boards that are thicker at one edge so they can overlap.

Clerestory Window.   A window set high on a wall just below the ceiling or roofline.

Closing.   The time when property is legally transferred from seller to buyer.

Cold Air Return.   In a forced warm air heating system, the registers and ducts that carry cool room air back to the furnace to be reheated.

Collar Tie.   A horizontal timber that connects two opposing roof rafters.

Come-along.   Hand-operated winch used to hold timbers or frame secure when erecting or dismantling a frame.

Concrete.   A hard, dense material made by mixing Portland cement, sand, and gravel with water. Used for footings, foundations, floors, and walks.

Concrete Block.   A building block made of concrete and used for foundation walls, piers, and outside walls. The standard block is 8 by 8 by 16 inches.

Construction Loan.   A short-term loan to cover the cost of building or renovation.

Contract for Sale.   Written agreement whereby buyer agrees to buy certain property the seller agrees to sell on the terms and conditions set forth in the contract. Also called "Agreement for Sale."

Cupola.   Structure set on top of a roof with louvers to allow warm air generated in the barn to escape. Cupolas on new barn houses are often quite large and have glass windows instead of wood louvers.

Decking.   2-by-4-inch boards suitable for outside wood decks, flooring, and roof boards.

Deed.   The document that when properly sealed and signed transfers ownership of property from seller to buyer.

Depth.   In framing, the thickness of a timber.

Dimensional Lumber.   Usually refers to lumber 1¾ inches thick and up to 15½ inches wide.

Dormer Window.   A window set in a small gable that projects from a roof.

Douglas Fir.   Species of evergreen growing in the Northwest and used for post-and-beam as well as stud construction.

Dovetail Joint.   Consists of fan-shaped tenon that fits into a mortise of similar shape.

Dry Rot.   Caused by a fungus that invades timbers, causing wood to become dry and powdery and eventually to weaken.

Drywall.   Interior wall panels made with a core of gypsum plaster encased in thick paper. The standard panel is 4 by 8 feet and ⅝ or ½ inch thick. Also called "Gypsum Wallboard," "Plasterboard," "Sheetrock," and "Wallboard."

Duct.   Round or rectangular pipe used in a forced warm air heating system to carry air heated in the furnace to room registers. Also used in central air-conditioning systems.

Dutch Barn.   See *New World Dutch Barn.*

Easement. Legal right granted to one individual to use a portion of another's land, such as a right-of-way.

Eaves. The edges of a roof that project beyond the walls.

Electric Service Entrance. Pipes and fittings that carry electric power from utility company lines into a house. Includes electric meter, main switch, and circuit breaker panel or fuse box. Also called "Service Entrance."

Encumbrance. A legal claim or judgment attached to property that would adversely affect the title.

English Barn. The so-called New England Barn—a simple and classic wood frame barn.

Epoxy Cement. A strong adhesive in liquid or paste form, used to repair timbers damaged by rot.

Escrow Agent. Neutral third party authorized by buyer and seller to handle the transfer of property.

Fiberglass. Insulating material made of glass fibers, used for walls, roofs, etc.

Fieldstone. Irregularly shaped stones used for foundations, walls, and fireplaces. These were the stones removed by farmers as they cleared their fields for plowing.

Floor Beam. Timber that supports the floorboards. Also called "Joist."

Footing. The relatively wide, thick section of concrete that supports the foundation of a building.

Foundation. A wall made of stone, concrete, block, or poured concrete resting on the footings and supporting the building.

Framing. Assembled timbers that form the structure of a building. Also the installation of the frame.

Fresh Air Exchanger. See *Air-to-air Heat Exchanger.*

Frost Line. The depth to which earth freezes in cold weather.

Fuel-fired. A system used to generate heat by burning fuels such as coal, gas, oil, or wood.

Furnace. Enclosure used to generate heat by the combustion of various fuels.

Furring. Wood strips nailed to a solid surface to produce an even nailing base, or to set two surfaces apart.

Gable. The triangular end of a building, formed by the eaves and ridge of a sloped roof.

Gambrel Roof. A roof with two slopes, the lower having a steeper slope than the upper.

General Contractor.   An individual experienced in handling all phases in the construction of a building.

Girder.   Heavy timber or steel beam that supports the floor beams at midpoint in their span.

Girt.   Horizontal timber that connects posts.

Grade.   The ground that surrounds a building.

Gusset.   A strip of wood or metal used to reinforce a joint or portion of a structure.

Gypsum Wallboard.   See *Drywall.*

Half-lap Joint.   A right-angle joint made by cutting notches in a timber to half the depth of the wood. After joining, the two pieces are secured with peg, tenon, bolt, or long nails.

Hand-Hewn.   Timbers shaped to size by hand with an adz or broadax.

Hardwood.   Wood from broad-leaved deciduous trees such as birch, hickory, maple, and oak.

Heel.   Lower end of a roof rafter that rests on the plate, or girt, on top of the wall.

House Wrap.   See *Air Infiltration Barrier.*

Hydronic Heat.   See *Circulating-Hot-Water Heat.*

Insulation.   Materials having a high resistance to the passage of heat.

Joinery.   Use of wood joints and pegs to connect timbers.

Joist.   A timber that frames the floor. Also called "Floor Beam."

Kiln-Dried.   Lumber that has been dried and seasoned in a large oven— a kiln.

Knee Brace.   A timber set diagonally between a vertical post and a horizontal beam or girt to provide additional support to the joint. Sometimes called by its English term, "Wind Brace."

Knee Wall.   A relatively low wall running between the top floor and the roof.

Lally Column.   A steel pipe filled with concrete and used in place of a wood post to support a horizontal beam or girder.

Layout.   Arrangement of space in a building. Also the drawing of a joint on a timber.

Lien.   A claim placed against property as security for an outstanding debt.

Lintel.   A beam of wood or metal over a door or window opening to support the wall above.

Lot.   A piece of land suitable for building.

Louvers.   Slanted thin boards set in a frame in a window or door opening to provide light and ventilation and keep out rain. Sometimes movable, sometimes fixed.

Low-E Glass (Low-emissivity glass).   Glass for windows and skylights engineered to reduce heat loss at night through the glass but allow the sun's heat to enter house.

Masonry Thermal Storage.   A wall or floor of thick masonry used to store the sun's heat in a passive solar system.

Master Carpenter.   A versatile and highly skilled craftsman.

Mechanic's Lien.   A claim placed against the property by one who has supplied labor and/or materials to improve the property.

Mortar.   Usually refers to a mixture of Portland cement, sand, and water that binds units of masonry together.

Mortise.   Notch or slot cut in a timber into which fits a tenon cut on another timber.

Mortise-and-Tenon Joint.   An interlocking joint where the tenon—a projection shaped at the end of one timber—is inserted into the mortise cut in the adjoining timber.

New World Dutch Barn.   Style of barn originated by early Dutch settlers in this country. Characterized by a steeply pitched roof.

Nominal Size.   Dimensions of a piece of lumber before it has been dressed to size. A 2-by-4—nominal size—actually measures 1½ by 3½ inches or so after it has been dressed.

Nonbearing Wall.   A wall that does not bear any weight of a floor or roof and therefore can be removed without the need of additional structural support.

Octagonal Barn.   An eight-sided barn.

Orientation.   Position of a building related to the four points of the compass.

Oriented Strand Board (OSB).   Building panels made of compressed wood particles and a binding agent. Similar to "Chipboard" and "Waferboard," but with superior nail-holding ability.

Overhang.   The portion of the roof that extends beyond the wall.

Parg.   A thin rough coat of mortar applied over a masonry wall. From *parget*, which means "plaster."

Partition.   An interior wall that separates rooms or divides space. Can be a bearing or a nonbearing wall.

Passive Solar Heat.   Solar heat provided by south-facing windows, skylights, and masonry thermal-storage walls and floors, and other non-mechanical methods.

Pennsylvania Dutch Barn. A sturdy and efficient barn style developed by early German settlers in Pennsylvania and adjoining areas. Often made of stone.

Percolation Test. A test made to determine how rapidly soil will absorb water. Required prior to installation of septic systems. Also called "Perc Test."

Pergola. An arbor or trellis used as an architectural element.

Pitch. The slope or angle of a roof.

Planning and Zoning Board. Department of local government charged with development and enforcement of regulations controlling use of land.

Plasterboard. See *Drywall.*

Plate. Horizontal timber running the length of a roof to support the heels of roof rafters. Also the top horizontal member of a stud wall.

Platform Framing. A type of stick-built or stud construction where each floor serves as a base or platform for framing the floor above.

Plumb Line. A cord with a weight on one end, used to determine if a post or wall is vertical—"plumb."

Plywood. Thin sheets of wood veneer glued together to produce strong building panels.

Post and Beam. Method of framing employing large timbers to produce a rigid structure. Also called "Timber Frame."

Powder Post Beetle. A wood-destroying insect that damages timbers in old barns. The larvae work within the wood but leave visible signs such as fine sawdust around the edges of holes.

Prairie Barn. Usually refers to early barns built in the Midwest with pronounced open peaks at each end of the roof to provide ventilation and with broad, low-pitched roofs.

Precut Lumber. Lumber that has been cut to exact size at a factory or woodworking shop.

Prefabrication. Building method where building elements are assembled at the factory, or on-site, before being erected in place. Also "Prefab."

Prefab Metal Chimney. Metal flue encased by a metal cover with insulation between. Suitable for fireplaces, wood stoves, and other fuel-fired heating equipment. Requires no foundation, so is less costly and is easier and quicker to install than a masonry chimney.

Pressure-treated Lumber.   Wood treated with chemical preservatives applied under pressure to protect against rot and insects.

Pressure-wash.   The application of a cleaning solution under pressure through a hose to remove dirt from interiors of old barns and other buildings.

Principal Rafter.   Roof rafter framed into a bent.

Purlin.   Horizontal timber that gives support to roof rafters at their mid-point. May also connect pairs of rafters together.

Queen Posts.   Posts resting on top of bent girt that help support roof frame.

Radiant Heat.   Type of heat where objects are warmed rather than the air around the objects. Used in some forms of electric and circulating-hot-water heating systems.

Rafters.   Timbers that frame a roof and run from the top of a wall to the peak of the roof.

Real Estate Broker.   Person licensed by the state to sell land or buildings as well as to employ licensed agents or salespersons to sell under his or her supervision.

Restorationist.   Master carpenter or builder who specializes in the restoration of old structures.

Ridgepole.   Timber running the length of the roof to which the ends of rafters are secured. Also called "Ridgeboard."

Rigid Foam Panels.   Insulating material made of polyurethane or expanded polystyrene plastics.

Roof Boards.   Nailed to the top of roof rafters to serve as a nailing base for wood shingles.

Roughing-in.   Installation of basic plumbing and wiring.

R-value.   A measurement of the capacity of a specific material to resist passage of heat.

Saltbox.   Two-story house with a long, slanting roof that slopes to one story in the rear.

Septic System.   Underground tank, dry well, or leaching field used to handle household waste where there is no street sewer line.

Setback.   Distance a building must be set back from a road to comply with local zoning regulations.

Sheathing.   Solid covering applied to wall and roof frames to provide a nailing base for siding and roofing.

Shed Roof.   A roof with a single slope.

Sheetrock.   See *Drywall.*

Shell.   The complete exterior of a house—frame, sheathing, siding, windows, exterior doors, roofing, and subfloors.

Shingles.   Thin pieces of wood, slate, or asphalt roofing laid in overlapping rows on a roof.

Siding.   The material applied to the exterior of a house or barn.

Sills.   Timbers that rest on top of the foundation wall and serve as a base for the frame.

Silo.   A large cylindrical structure of wood, concrete, or masonry block adjoining the barn and used to store silage (fodder for cattle).

Softwood.   Lumber from evergreen trees such as fir, hemlock, or pine.

Solar Heat.   The sun's energy when used to heat buildings.

Span.   Unsupported distance of a horizontal beam connected at each end to posts.

Standing Seam Metal Roof.   Roof material made of prefinished metal plates connected by a raised seam to provide a watertight joint.

Stick-built.   Conventional method of construction using numerous pieces of small lumber—2-by-3, 2-by-4, 2-by-6—"sticks."

Stress-skin Panels.   Rigid building panels that combine drywall, insulation, and sheathing, used as exterior "wrapping" on a building.

Stud-built.   Same as "Stick-built."

Studding or *Studs.*   Vertical members of frame and interior walls in stick-built construction.

Stud Wall.   Any wall frame made with studding.

Subcontractor.   Firm or individual specializing in one aspect of building—masonry, plumbing, heating, wiring, and so forth.

Subfloor.   Boards or building panels nailed to floor beams or joists to serve as a base for finish flooring. Also called "Rough Floor."

Summer Beam.   A wood girder running the length of a building. It connects the tops of horizontal members of bents and can also serve as support for second-level floor beams.

Tenon.   Projection cut at one end of a timber to fit into a mortise cut in the adjoining timber.

Termites.   Small ground-nesting insects that chew wood in order to obtain cellulose, their principal food. Can do much damage.

Timber.   Any piece of lumber larger than 4 inches by 4 inches that is suitable for post-and-beam construction.

Timber Frame. Similar to post-and-beam but timbers are always connected with wood joinery and secured with wood pegs. Metal fasteners are not used.

Timber Framer. One who is skilled in the craft of timber frame construction.

Title. Evidence of ownership to property.

Title Insurance. Protects holder from loss due to any defect in title.

Tongue-and-groove. Wood joint where the projecting tongue formed along the edge of one board fits into a corresponding groove cut in the adjoining board. Often abbreviated as T&G. Commonly used on flooring and exterior siding.

Top Plate. The horizontal length of lumber or timber at the top of a wall frame.

Trombe Wall. A thick exterior wall of masonry covered with glass used to collect and provide heat with some passive solar systems.

Truss. Assembly of timbers that forms a rigid framework. A *bent* is a form of truss.

Vapor Barrier. Treated material applied to the inside face of an exterior wall or roof to prevent house-generated moisture vapor from reaching insulation.

Variance. An exception to a requirement of local zoning ordinances.

Waferboard. Building panels similar in composition to *chipboard*.

Wallboard. See *Drywall*.

Warranty Deed. The best kind of deed to receive because it includes a covenant that the seller will defend the title against any claimant.

Wind Barrier. See *Air Infiltration Barrier*.

Wood Joinery. Timbers joined with wood joints secured with wooden pegs.

Zoning Ordinances. Local regulations that control use of land.

Bibliography

Arthur, Eric, and Dudley, Witney. *The Barn: A Vanishing Landmark in North America*. New York: A&W Publishers, 1972.

Benson, Tedd. *Building the Timber Frame House*. New York: Charles Scribner's Sons, 1980.

———. *The Timber Frame Home*. Newtown, Conn.: The Taunton Press, 1988.

Burden, Ernest. *Living Barns: How to Find and Restore a Barn of Your Own*. New York: Bonanza Books, 1977. Reprint 1984.

Cobb, Hubbard. *How to Buy and Remodel the Older House*. New York: Macmillan Publishing Co., Inc., 1972.

Dickinson, Duo. *The Small House*. New York: McGraw-Hill Book Company, 1986.

Kelly, Frederick J. *Early Domestic Architecture in Connecticut*. New York: Dover, 1952.

Kidder, Tracy. *The House*. Boston: Houghton Mifflin, 1985.

Kinney, Jean, and Cle. *47 Creative Houses That Started as Bargain Buildings*. New York: Funk & Wagnalls, 1974.

Litchfield, Michael. *Renovations—A Complete Guide*. New York: McGraw-Hill Book Company, 1982.

Mazria, Edward. *The Passive Solar Energy Book*. Emmaus, Penn.: Rodale Press, 1979.

The R.S. Means Company. *Home Improvement Cost Guide*. Mount Vernon, N.Y.: Consumers Union, 1987.

Ramsey, Charles, and Sleeper, Harold. *Architectural Graphic Standards*. New York: John Wiley & Sons, 1970.

Schuler, Stanley. *American Barns: In a Class by Themselves*. Exton, Penn.: Schiffer Publishing, 1984.

Sloane, Eric. *An Age of Barns*. New York: Ballantine Books, 1974.

Sobon, John, with Schroder, Roger. *Timber Frame Construction*. Pownal, Ver.: Garden Way Publishing Company, 1984.

Taylor, Stephen. *A Place of Your Own Making*. New York: Henry Holt & Co., Inc., 1988.

Wade, Alex. *Alex Wade's Guide to Affordable Houses*. Emmaus, Penn.: Rodale Press, 1984.

Watkins, A. M. *The Complete Guide to Factory-Made Houses*. Chicago: Longman Financial Services Publishing, Inc., 1988.

Watson, Donald. *Climatic Design*. New York: McGraw-Hill Book Company, 1983.

Wissinger, Joanna. *The Best Kit Homes*. Distributed by Rodale Press. New York: The Philip Lief Group, Inc., 1987.

Youssef, Wasfi. *Building Your Own Home*. New York: John Wiley & Sons, 1988.

The New York State Barn Company (Box 146, RD #3, Canastota, New York 13032) has an extensive inventory of books on barns, farm buildings, timber framing, and so forth. For mail order, write for a listing of books.

Sources

Manufacturers of Standard and Custom Package Barn House Kits

(Package kits contain all materials required to erect an insulated, weathertight shell with windows, exterior doors, subflooring, and other components. Some packages also include finish materials such as trim, stairs, interior doors, and balconies.)

Habitat/American Barn. 123 Elm Street, South Deerfield, Massachusetts 01373.

Shelter-Kit Incorporated. Box 1, 22 Mill Street, Tilton, New Hampshire 03276.

Timberpeg. P.O. Box 474, West Lebanon, New Hampshire 03784.

Yankee Barn Homes. Star Route 3, Box 2, Grantham, New Hampshire 03753.

NOTE: Manufacturers of package kit houses in all sections of this country are listed in *The Complete Guide to Factory-Made Houses* and in *The Best Kit Homes*, which also includes Canadian manufacturers (see bibliography).

Post-and-Beam Frame Kits

(These kits are frames only, although some companies will supervise erection on through to the finished barn house.)

The Barn People. P.O. Box 217, Windsor, Vermont 05089.

The Beamery. 620 Bull Run Valley, Heiskell, Tennessee 37754.

Benson Woodworking Company, Inc. Box 22, Pratt Road, RR #1, Alstead Center, New Hampshire 03602.

Houses and Barns by John Libby. Barn Masters, Inc. P.O. Box 258, Freeport, Maine 04032.

Pacific Post and Beam. P.O. Box 13708, San Luis Obispo, California 93406.

Craig Rowley Restorations Ltd. 29 Reidy Hill Road, Amston, Connecticut 06231.

The Shelter Institute. 38 Center Street, Bath, Maine 04530.

NOTE: Timber framers in many sections of this country make up house and barn house frames. Check your local area.

Associations

Stress-skin Panels

Structural Insulated Panel Association. 1090 Vermont Avenue, Washington, D.C. 20035. Write for the list of panel manufacturers to locate one that serves your area.

Timber Framers Guild of North America. P.O. Box 1046, Keene, New Hampshire 03431. Write for a complete list of members and the professional directory that contains photos and descriptions of many timber frame firms all over the country.

Hands-on Courses and Workshops in House Construction

Heartwood. Johnson Hill Road, Washington, Massachusetts 01235.
The Owner-Builder Center. 1516 5th Street, Berkeley, California 94710.
The Shelter Institute. 38 Center Street, Bath, Maine 04530.

NOTE: State community colleges sometimes offer courses in home construction and some timber framers provide hands-on courses in the art of timber framing.

Plans

Ashland Barns. 990 CL, Butlercreek, Ashland, Oregon 95720. Plans for 82 barns, minibarns, garages, and craft shops. Comprehensive catalog, $5 (refundable).
Homestead Design. P.O. Box 998, Friday Harbor, Washington 98250. Catalog contains wide selection of plans plus helpful booklet, "The Homestead Design Construction Primer," $5.

Product Catalogs

Real Good. 966-H Mazzoni Street, Ukiah, California 95482 (1-800-688-9288). Free 104-page catalog of energy-saving products and 320-page book of 1,000 energy-saving ideas for $10 (refundable).

Renovator's Supply. Miller Falls, Massachusetts 01349. Reproductions of antique hardware, plumbing, and electrical fixtures.

Solar Components Corp. 121 Valley Road, Manchester, New Hampshire 03103. Extensive listing of a wide selection of solar products.

Real Estate Catalogs

(These contain many listings of farms with houses and barns.)

United National Real Estate. 40700 Belleview, Kansas City, Missouri 64112 (1-800-999-1020).

Strouts, P.O. Box 4528, Springfield, Missouri 65808 (1-800-555-1212).

Periodicals

Country Journal. P.O. Box 8200, Harrisburg, Pennsylvania 17105.

Fine Homebuilding magazine. The Taunton Press, Inc., Newtown, Connecticut 06470.

Historic Preservation. National Trust for Historic Preservation, 1785 Massachusetts Avenue, Washington, D.C. 20036.

Newtown Bee. 5 Church Hill Road, Newtown, Connecticut 06470.

Old House Journal. 435 Ninth Street, Brooklyn, New York 11215.

INDEX